Coloring Book for Kids

Legend ART

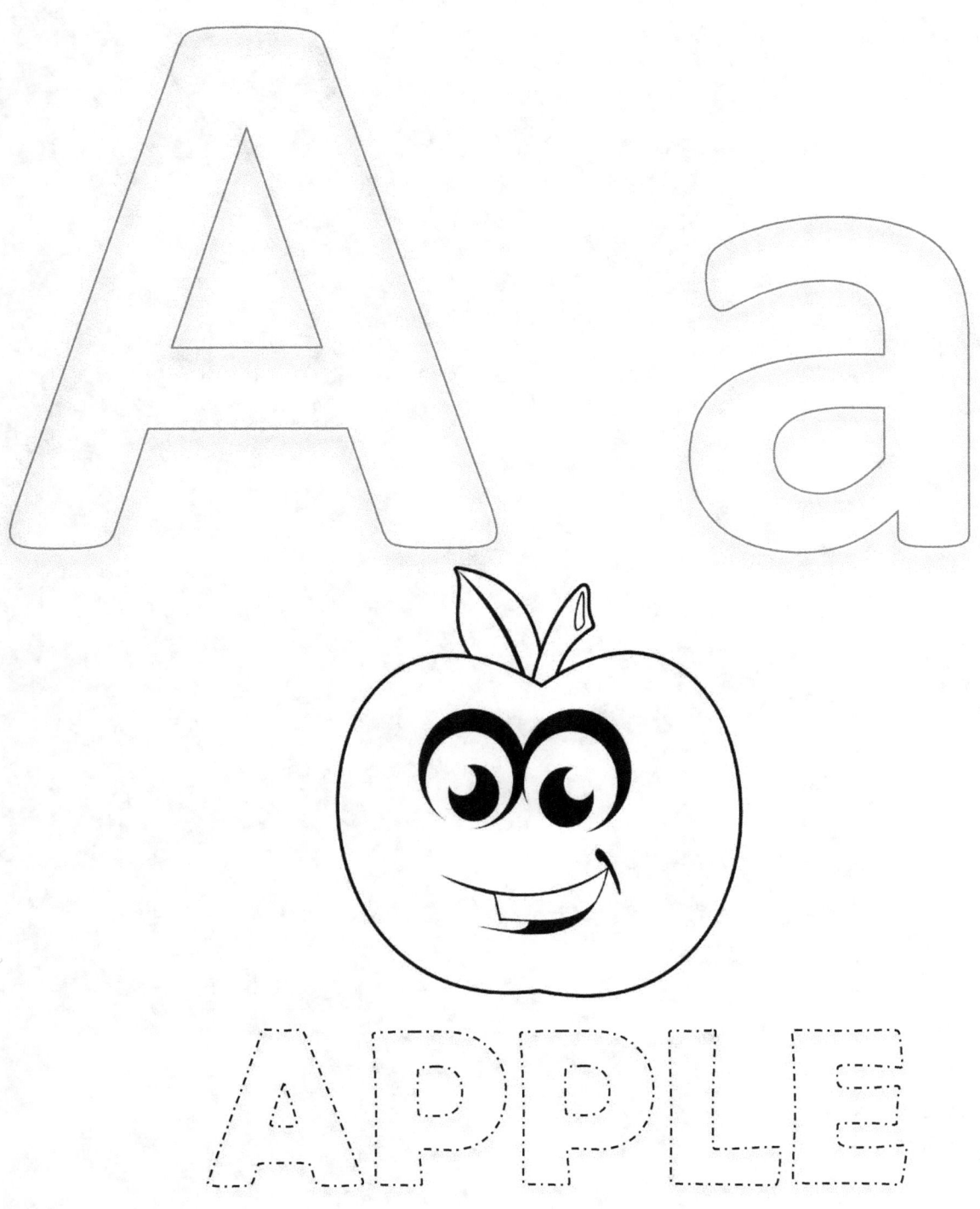

B b

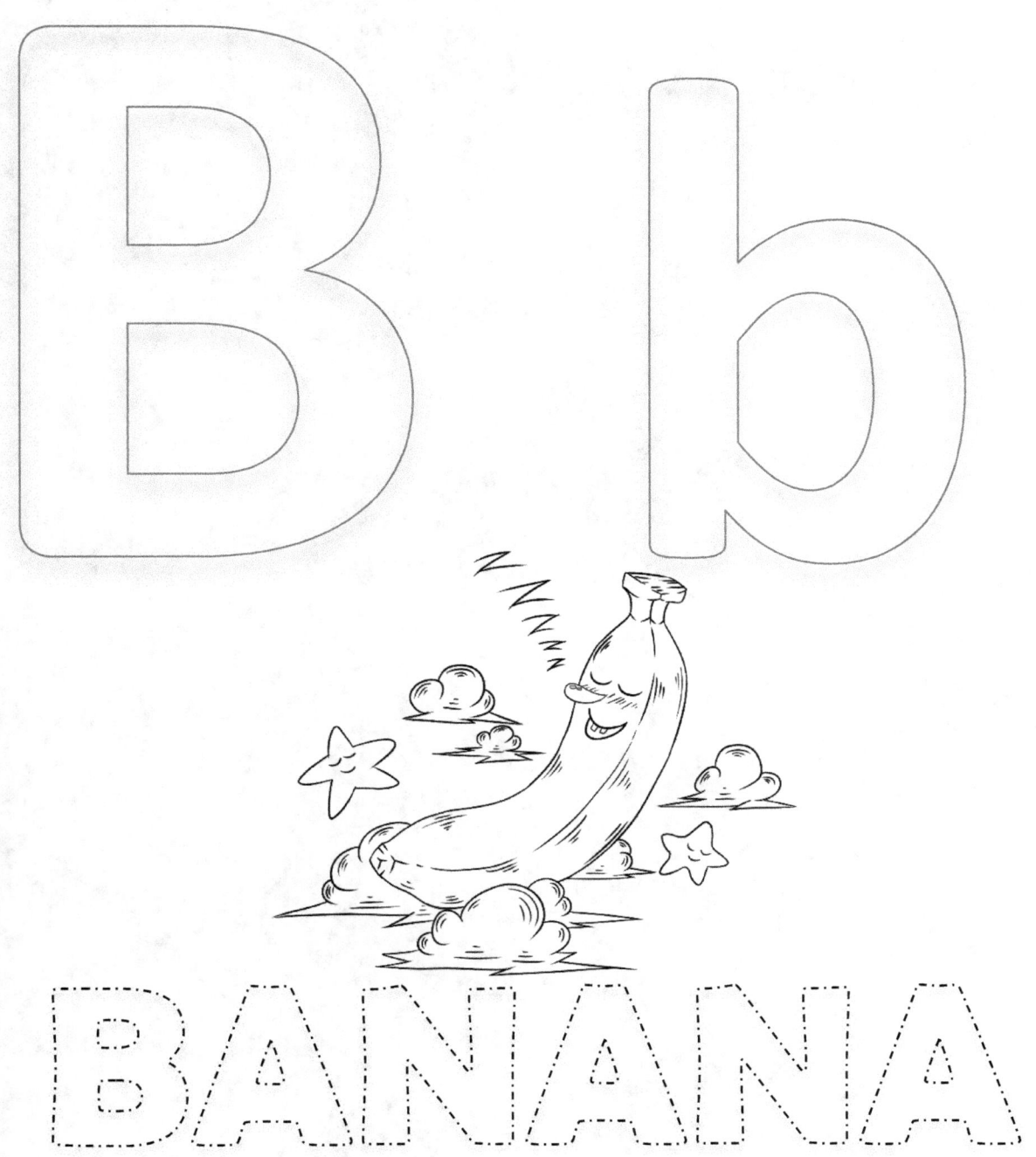

BANANA

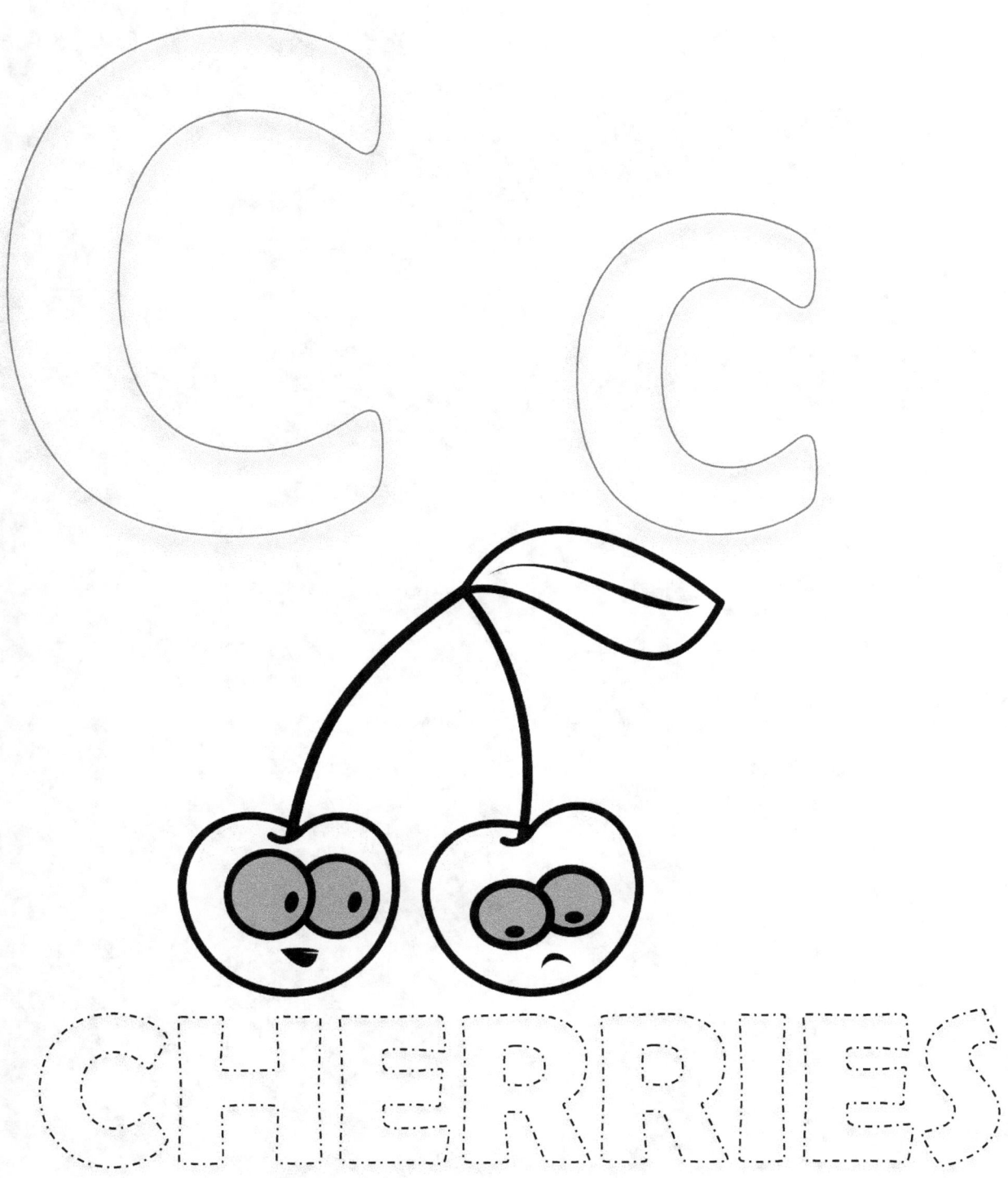

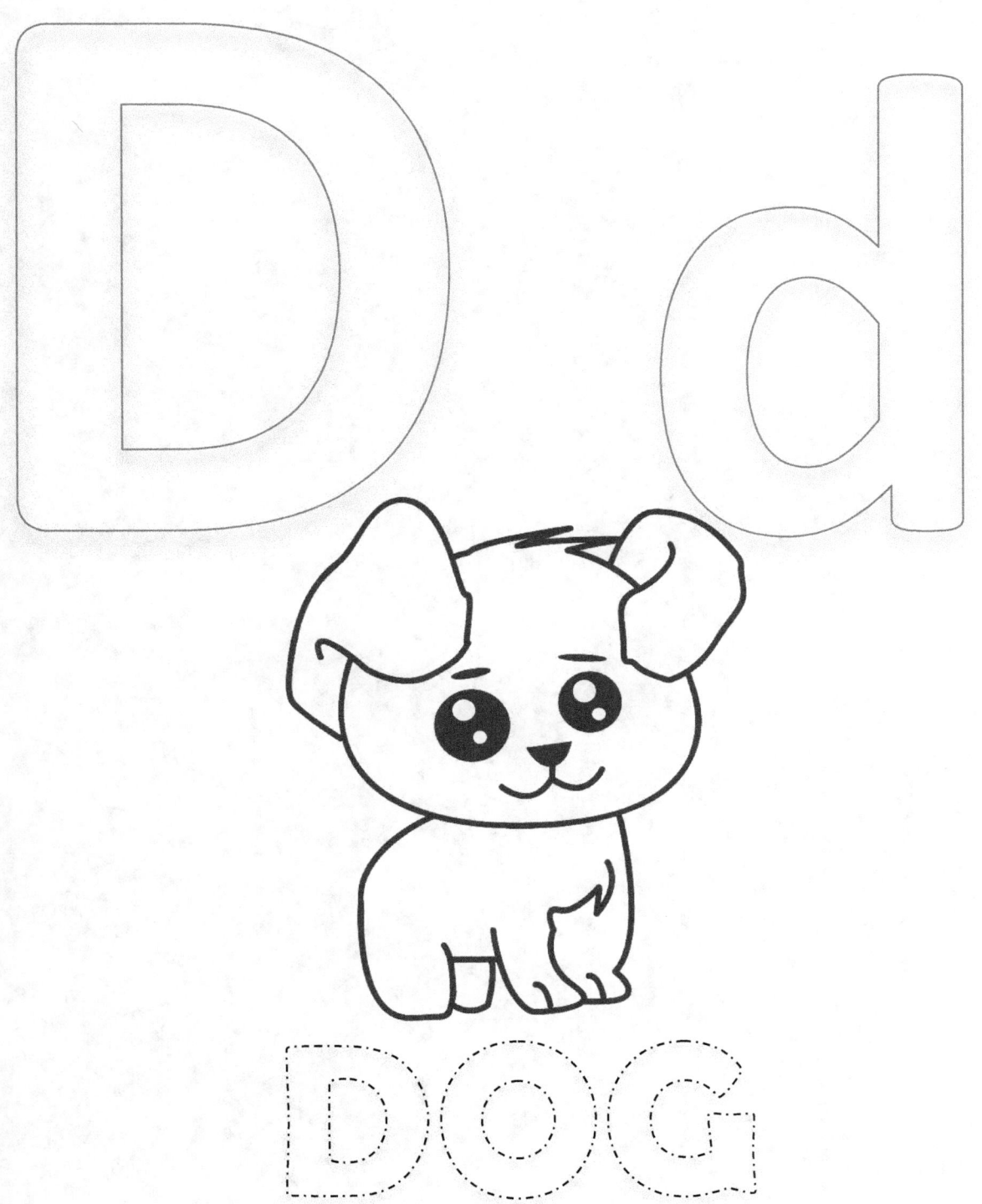

x

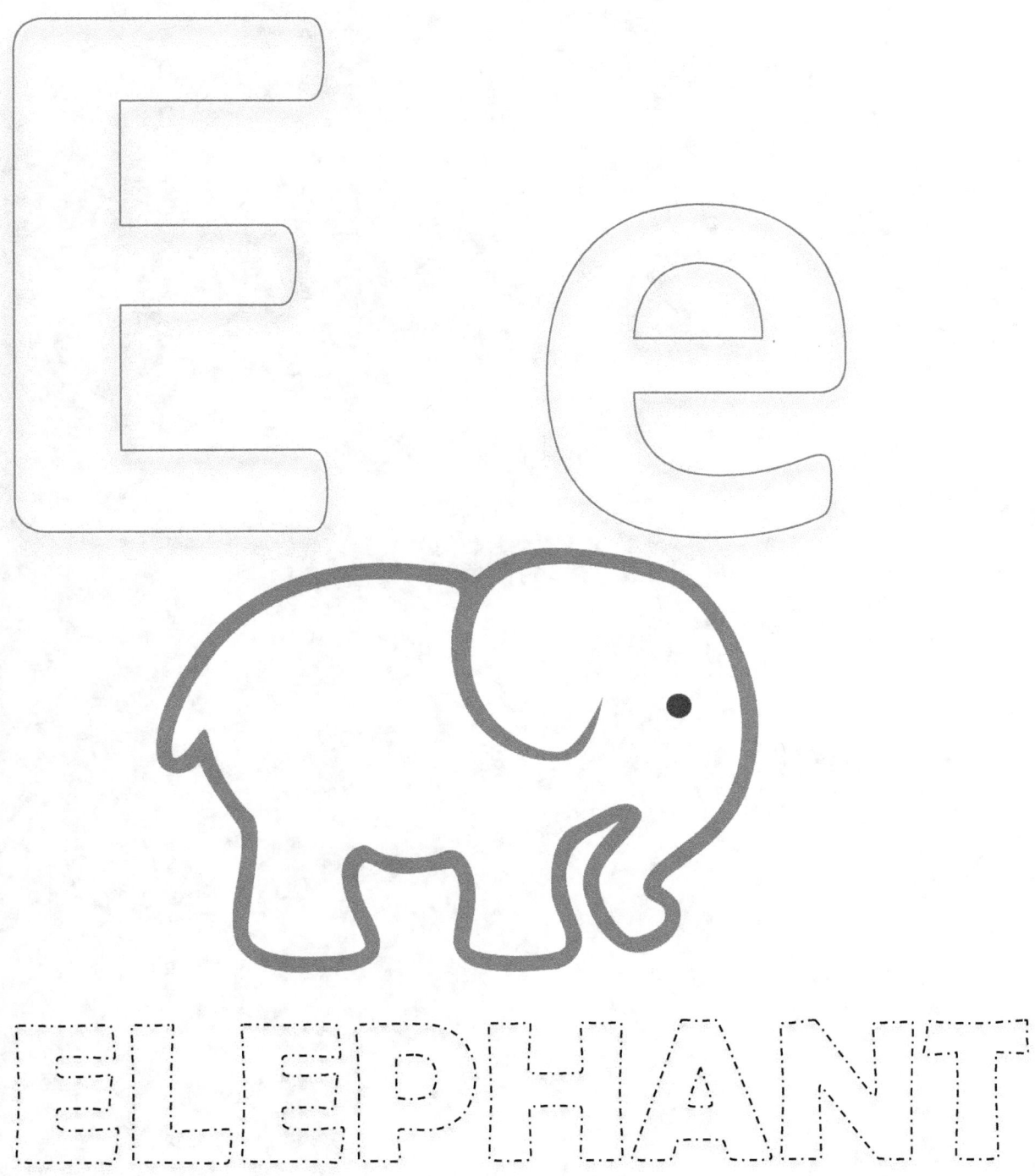

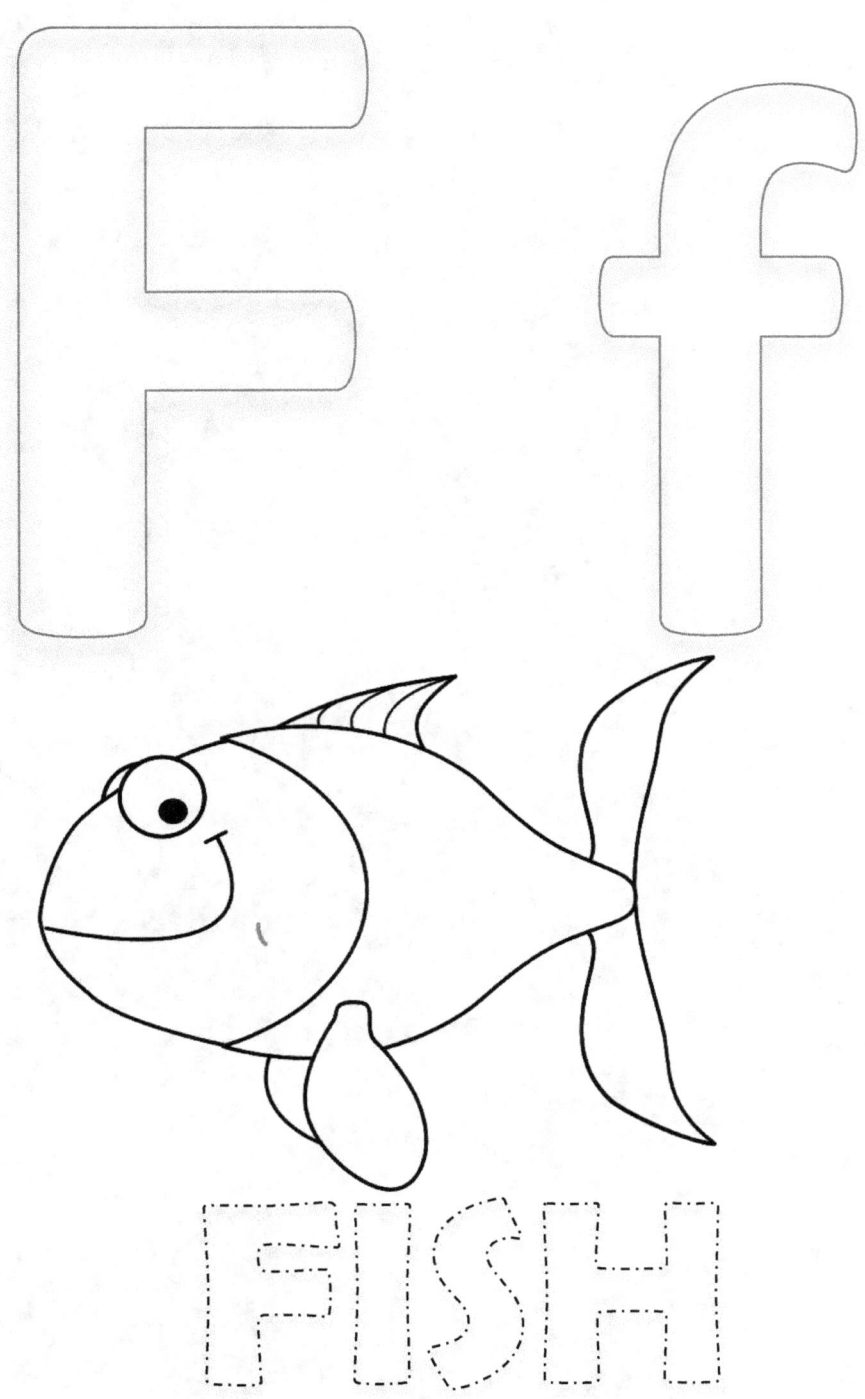

Gg

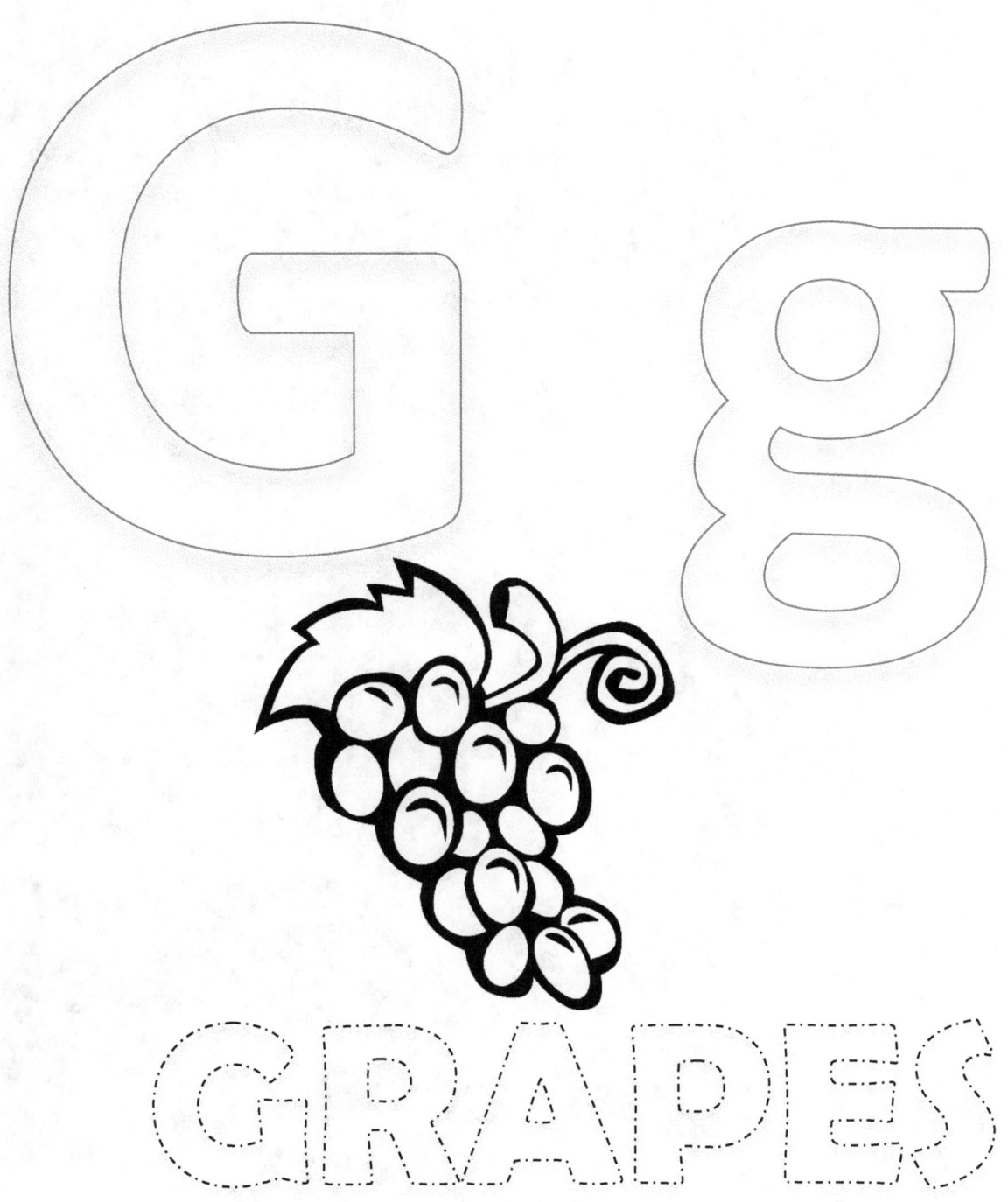

GRAPES

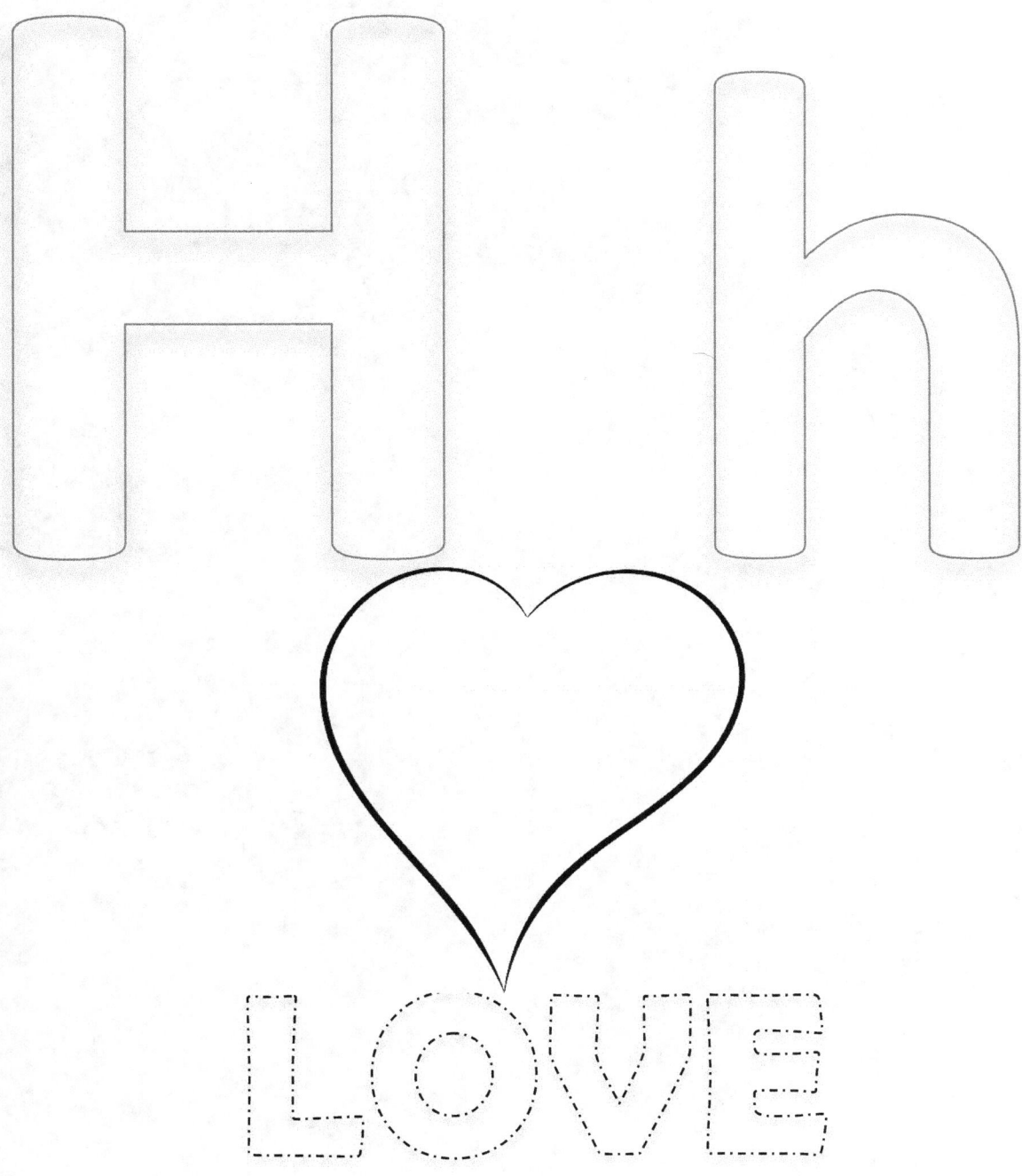

I i

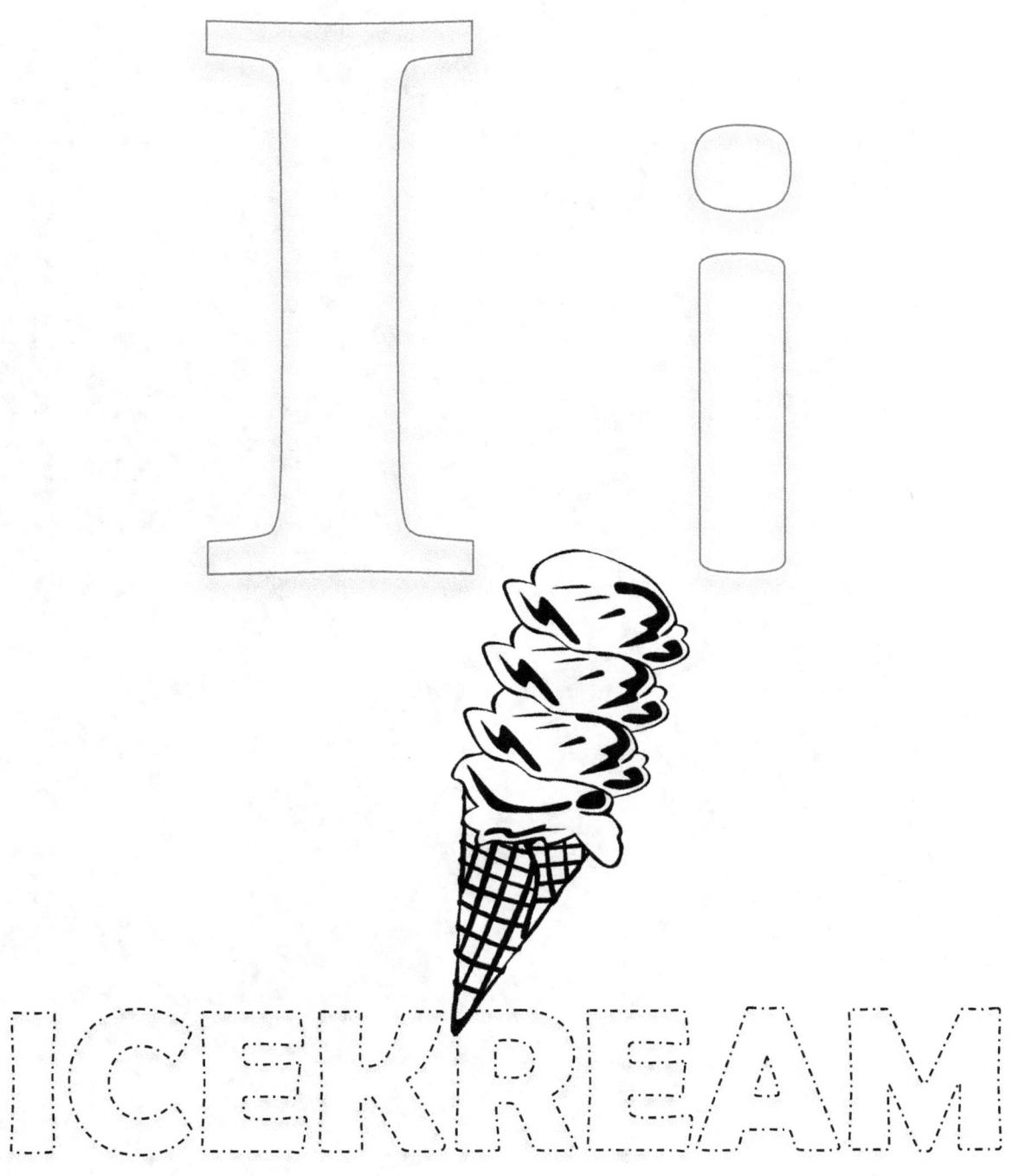

ICEKREAM

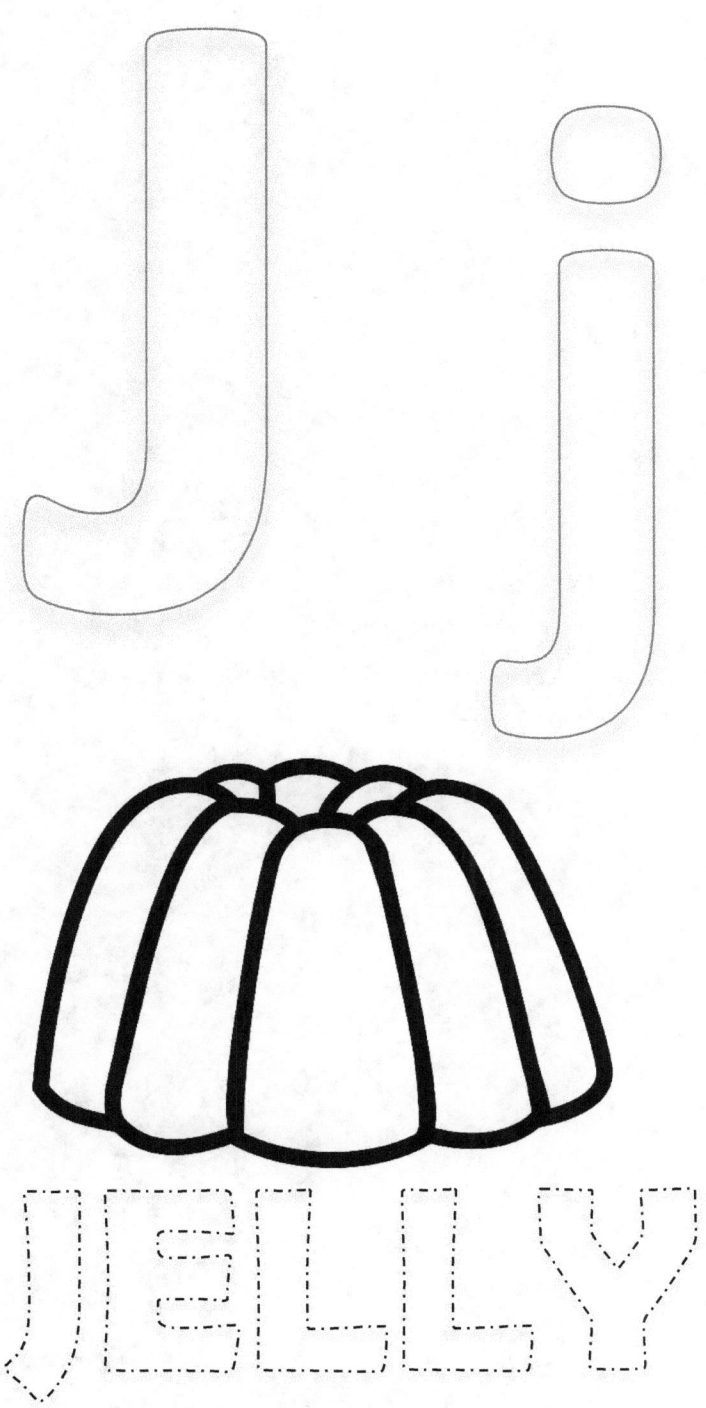

K k

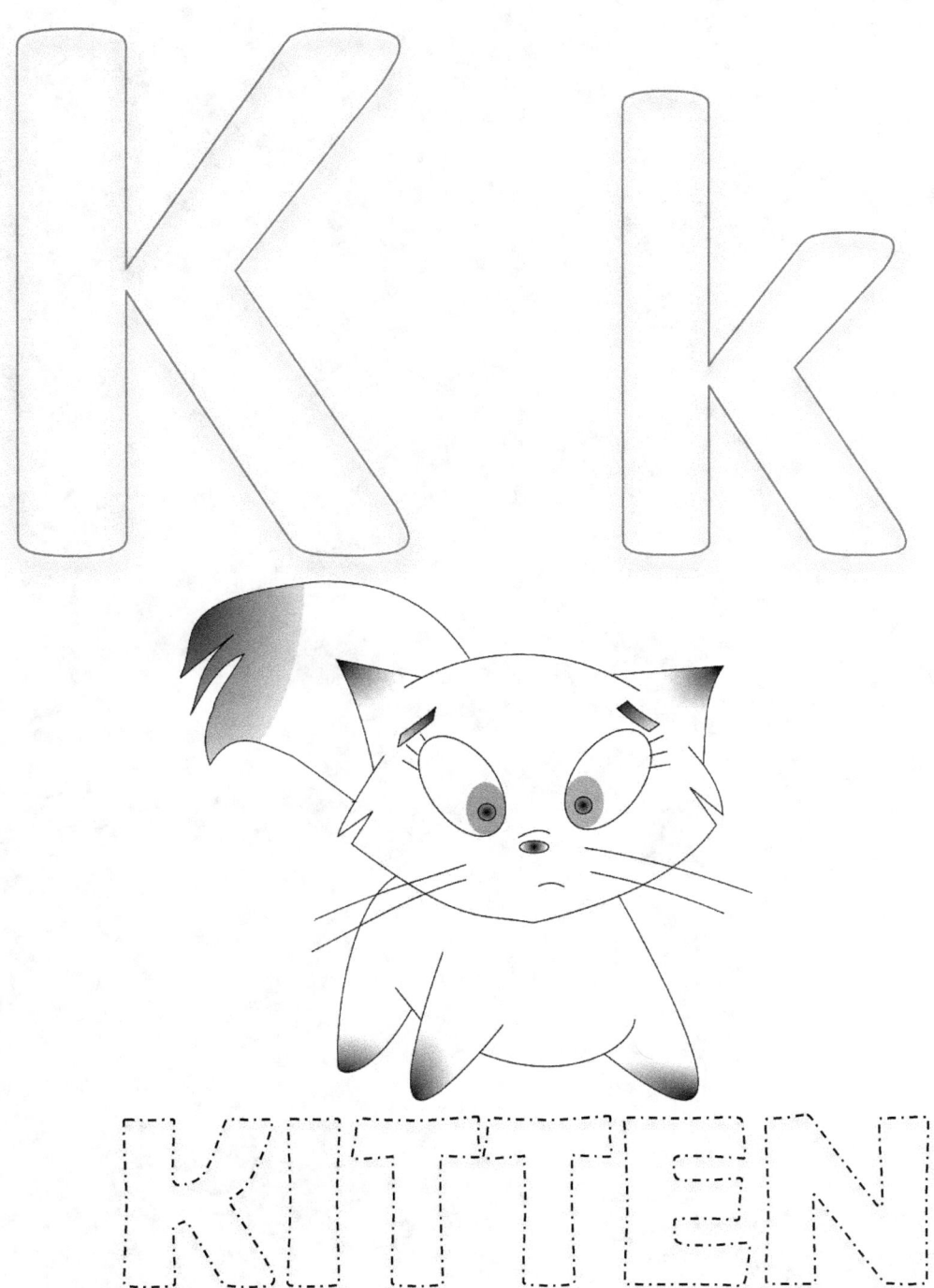

KITTEN

Ll

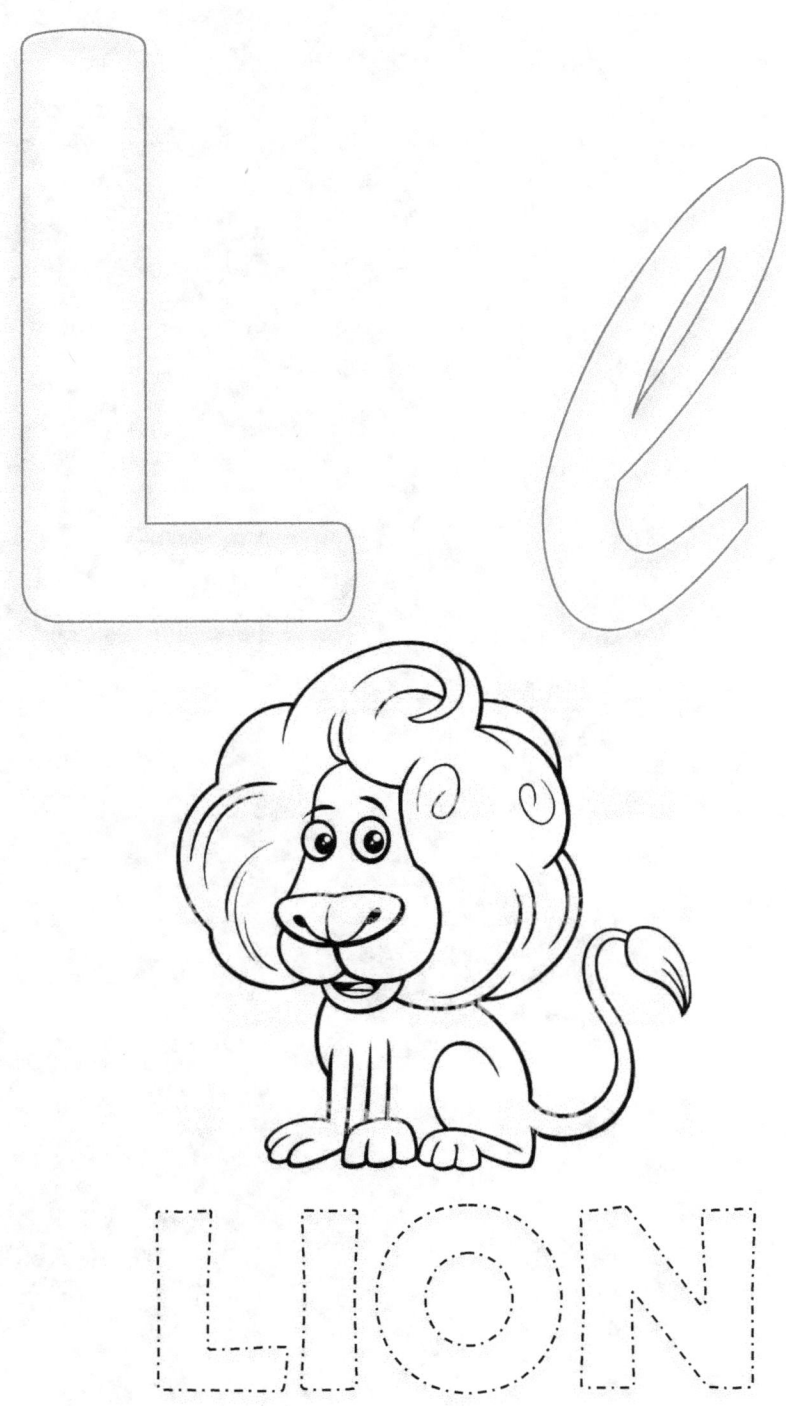

LION

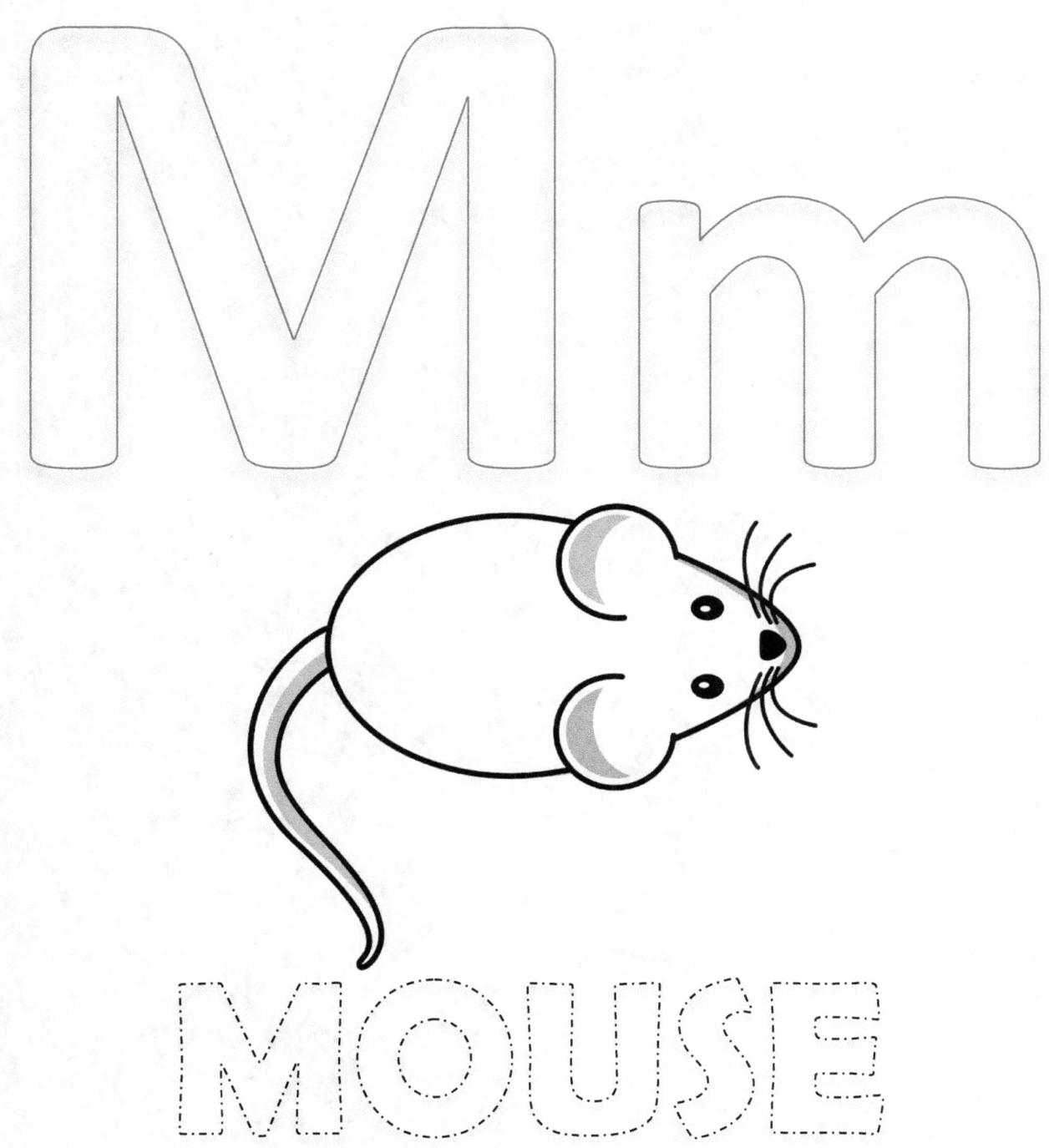

N n

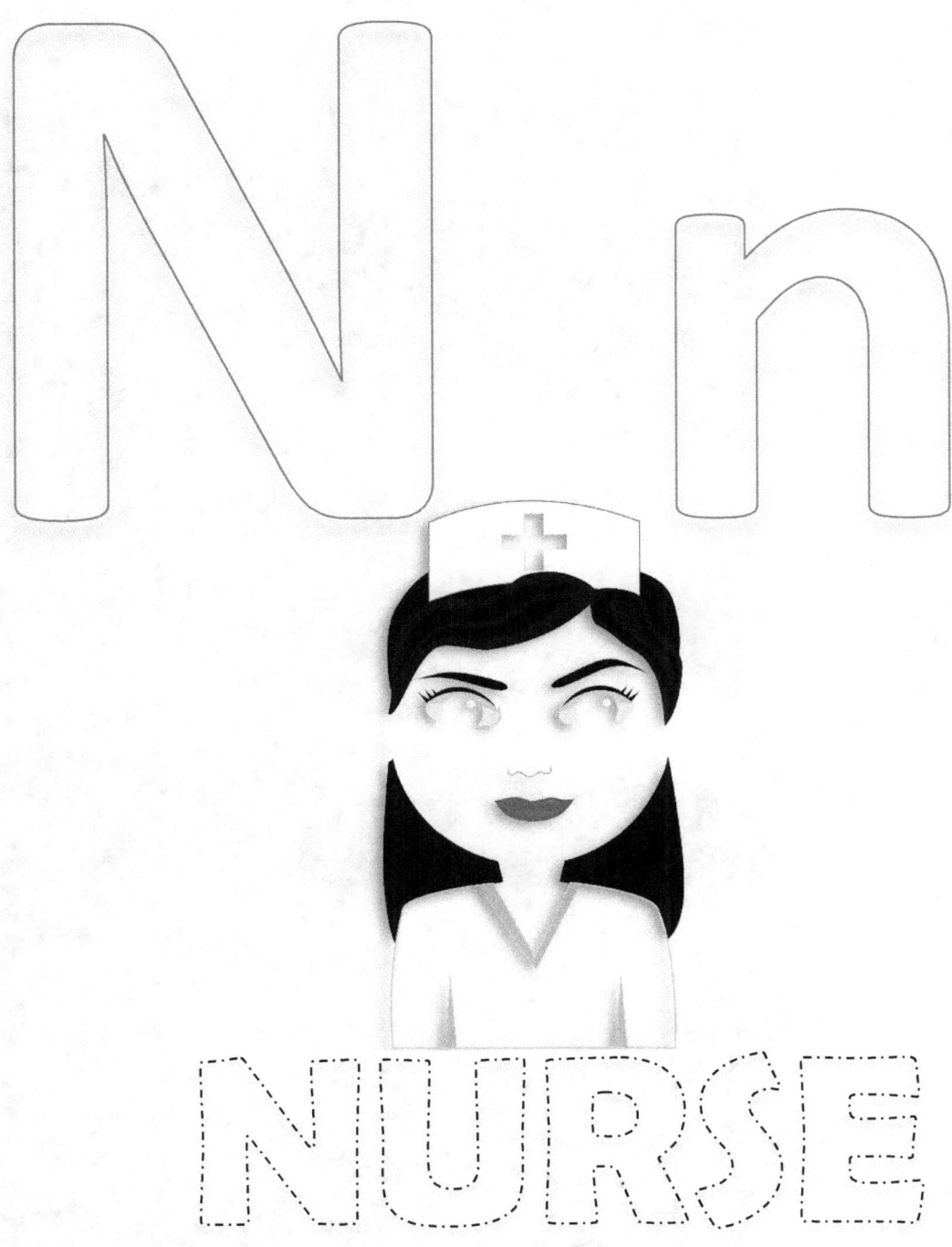

NURSE

xxx

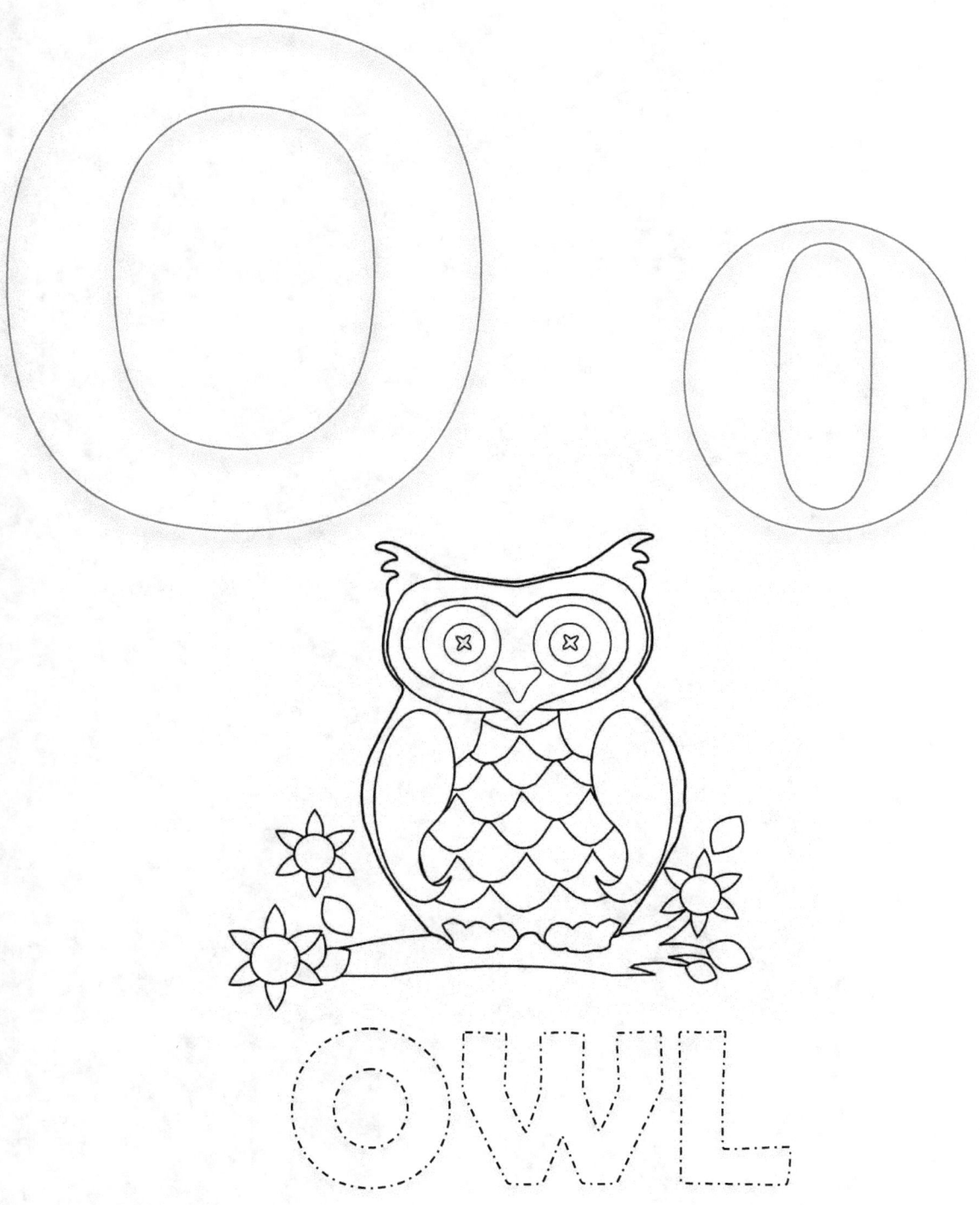

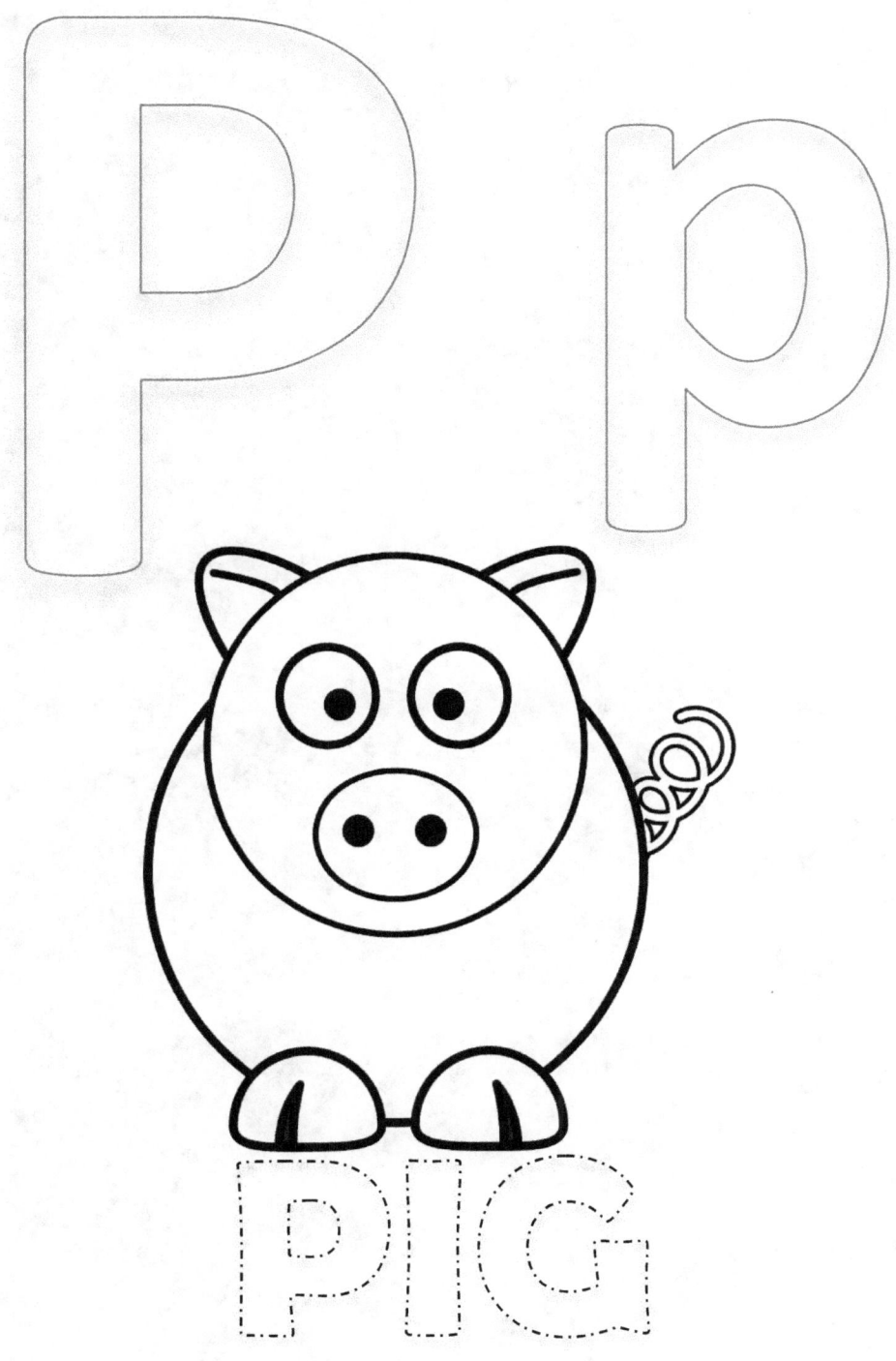

Qq

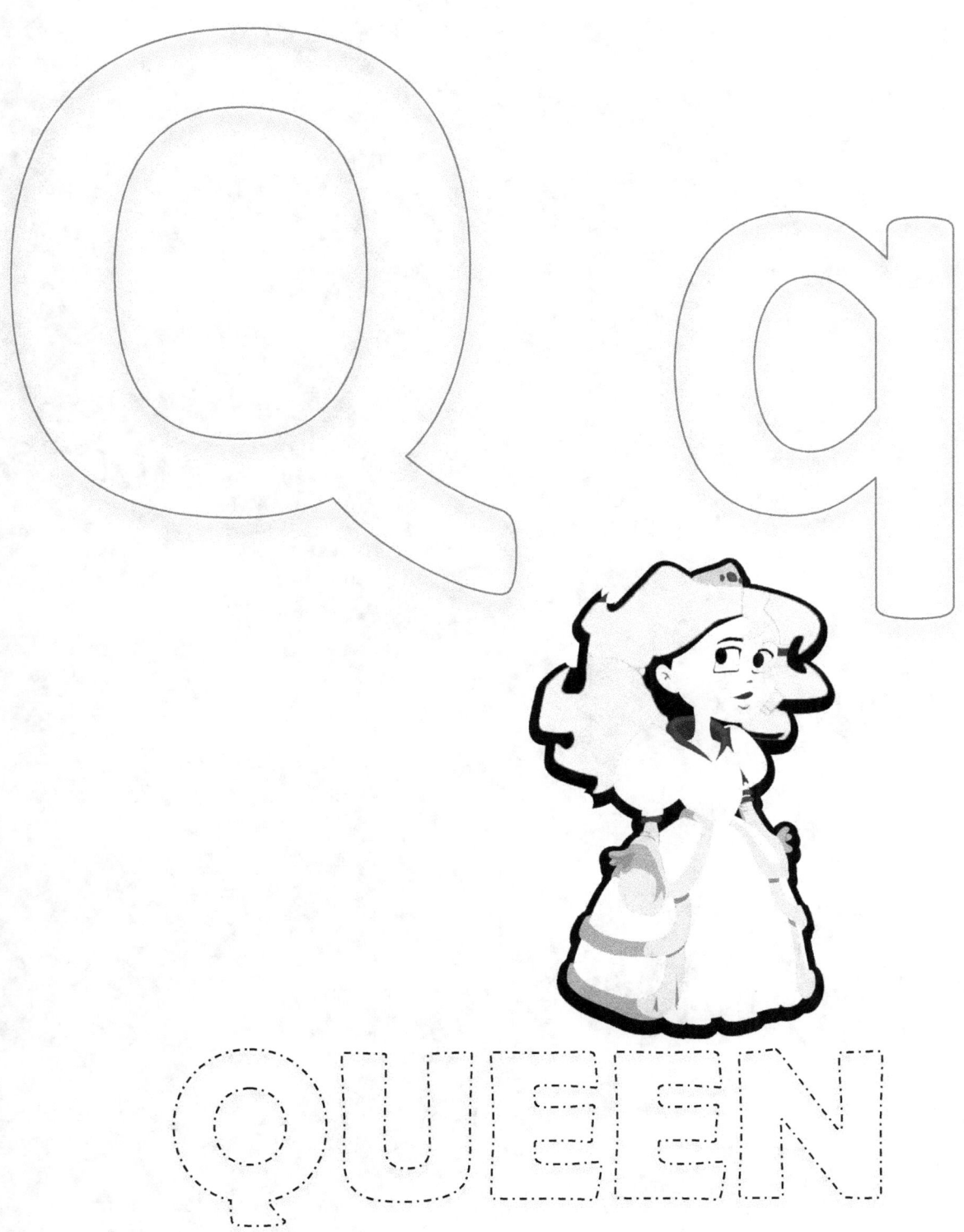

QUEEN

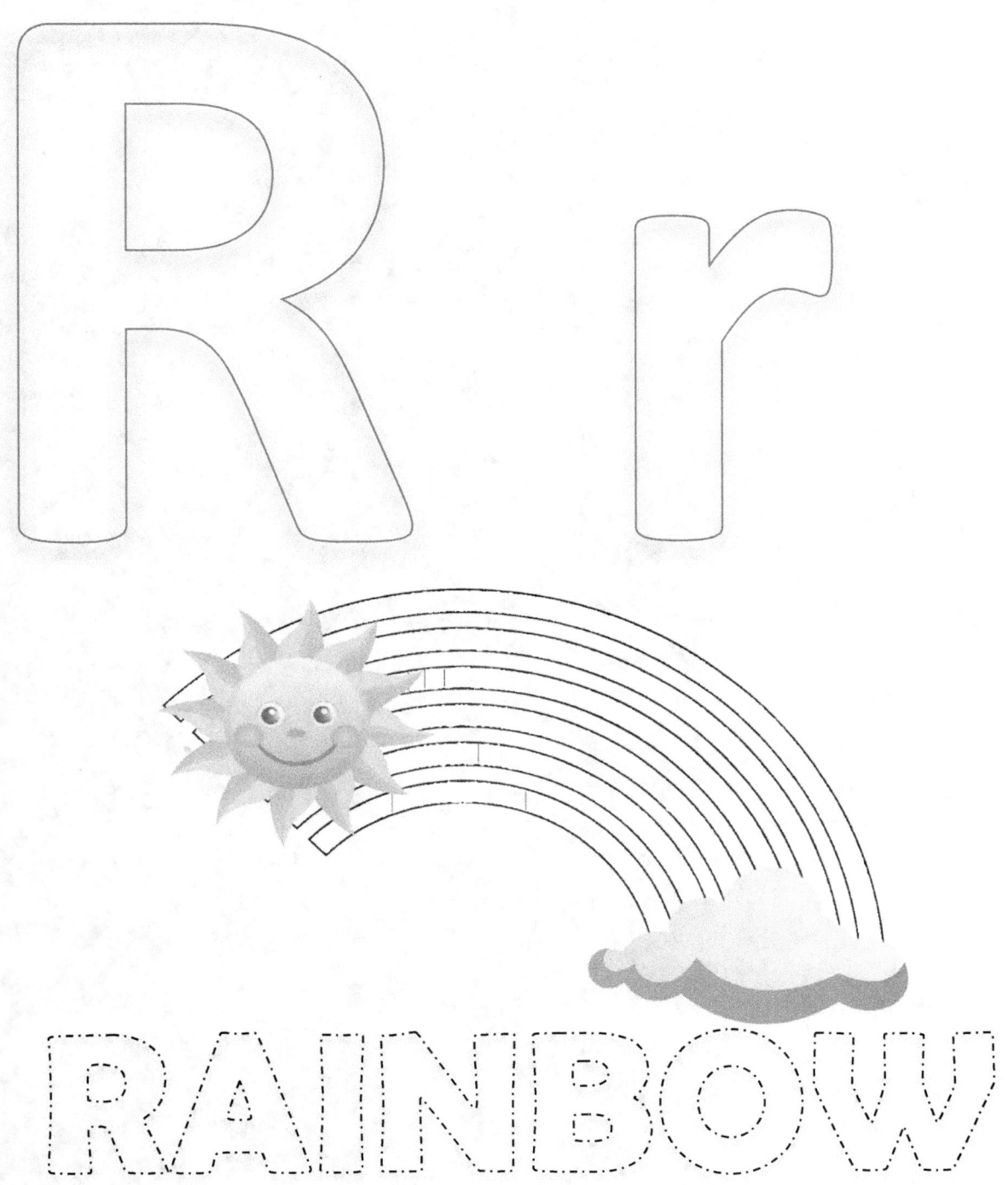

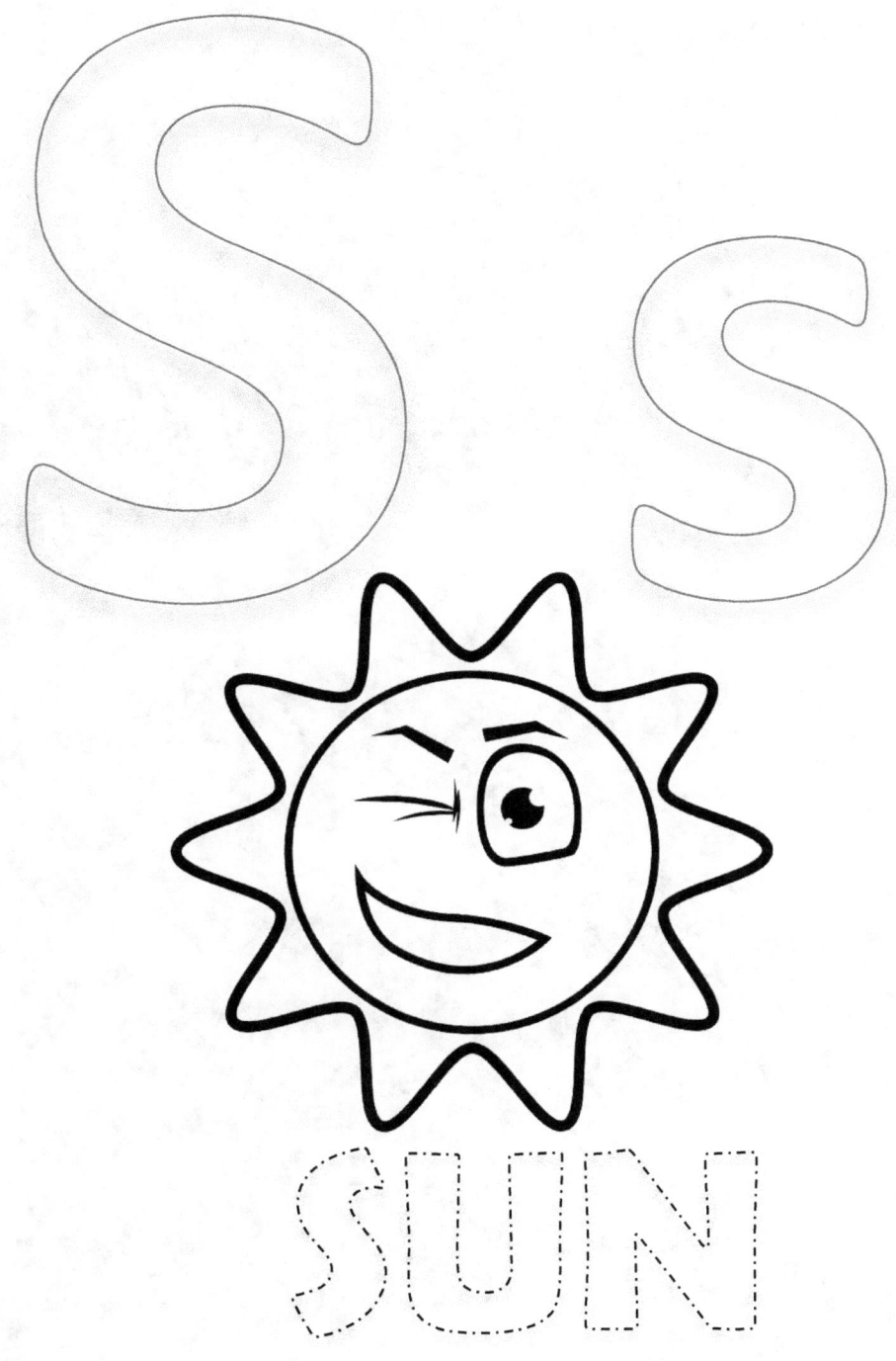

xl

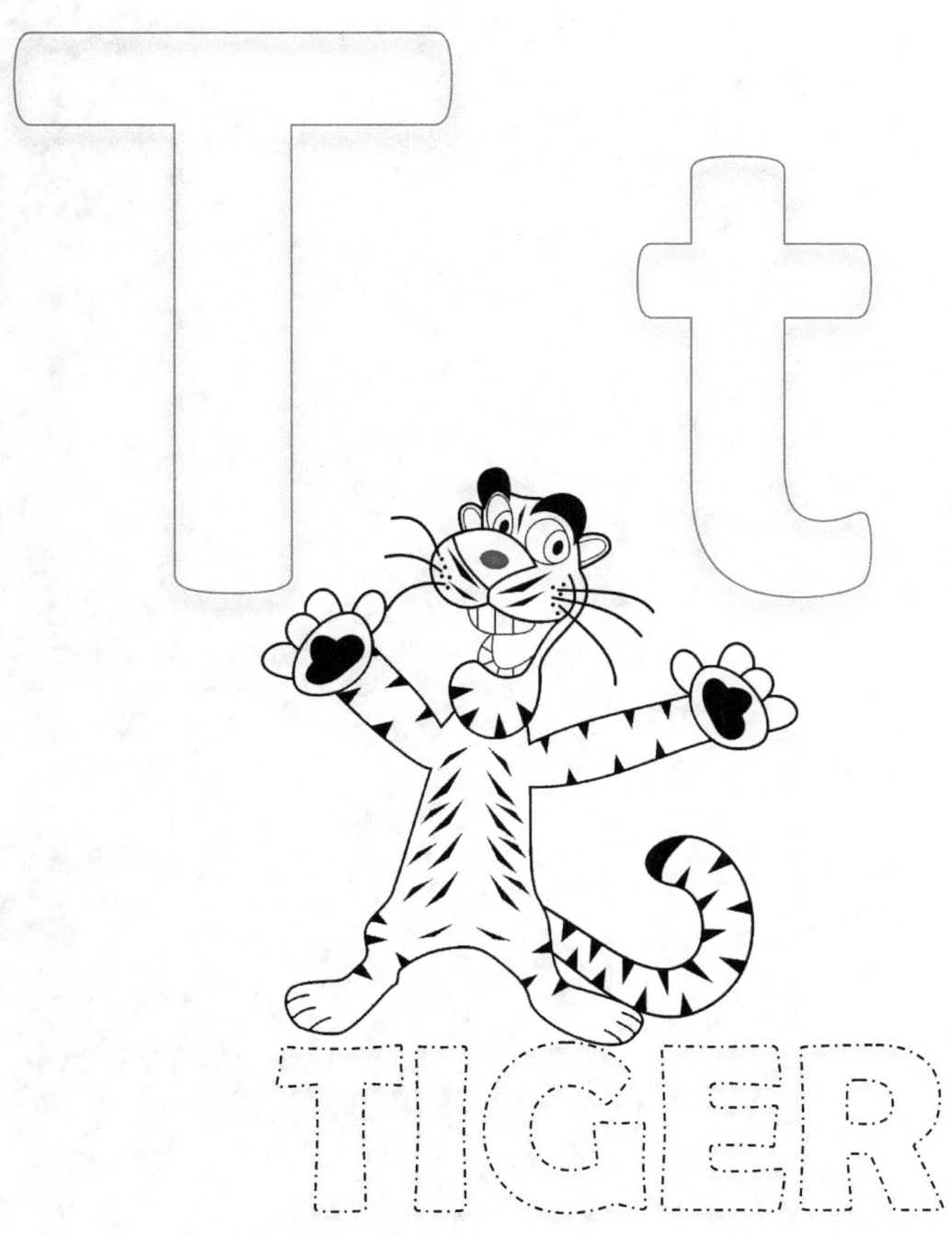

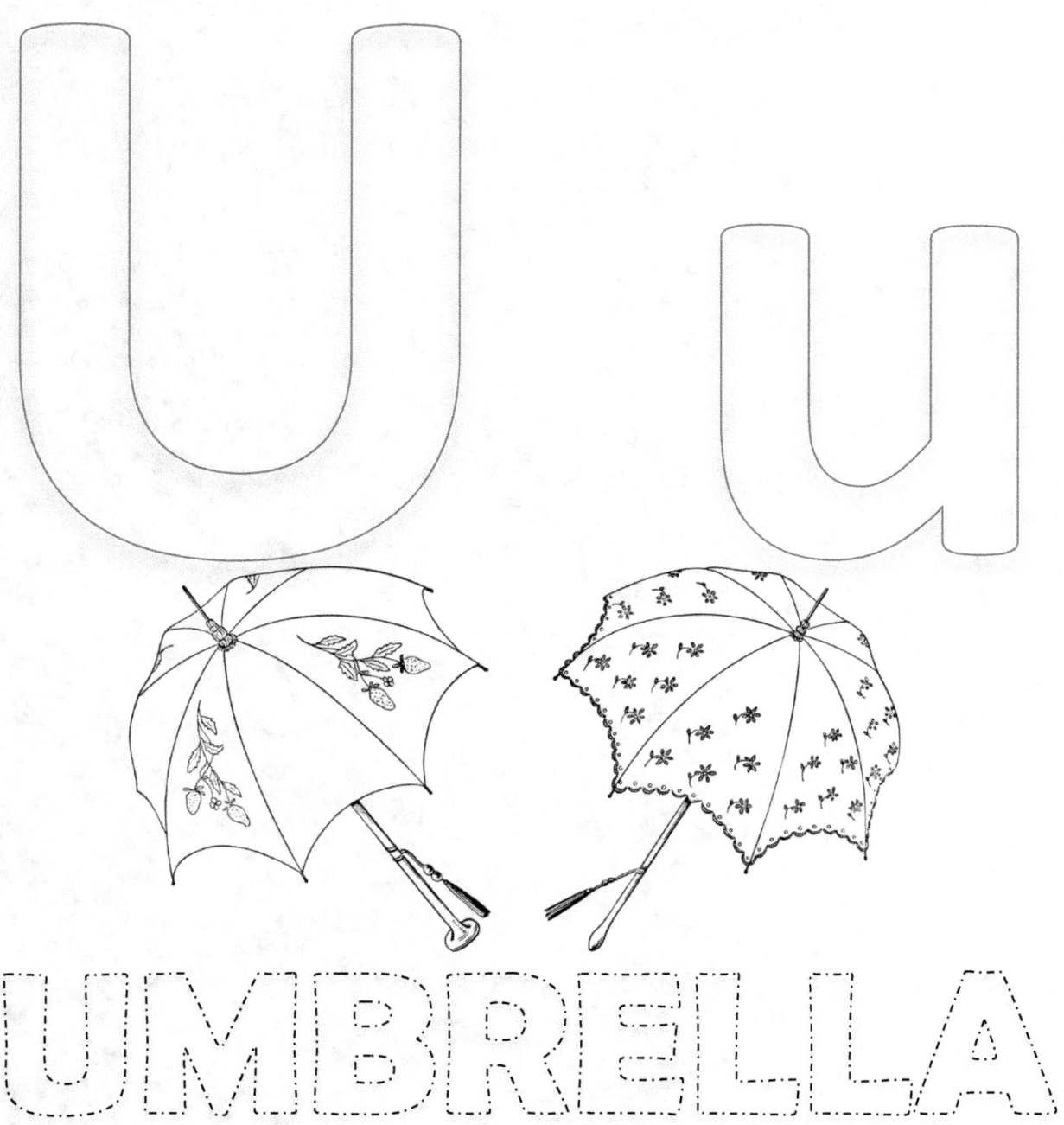

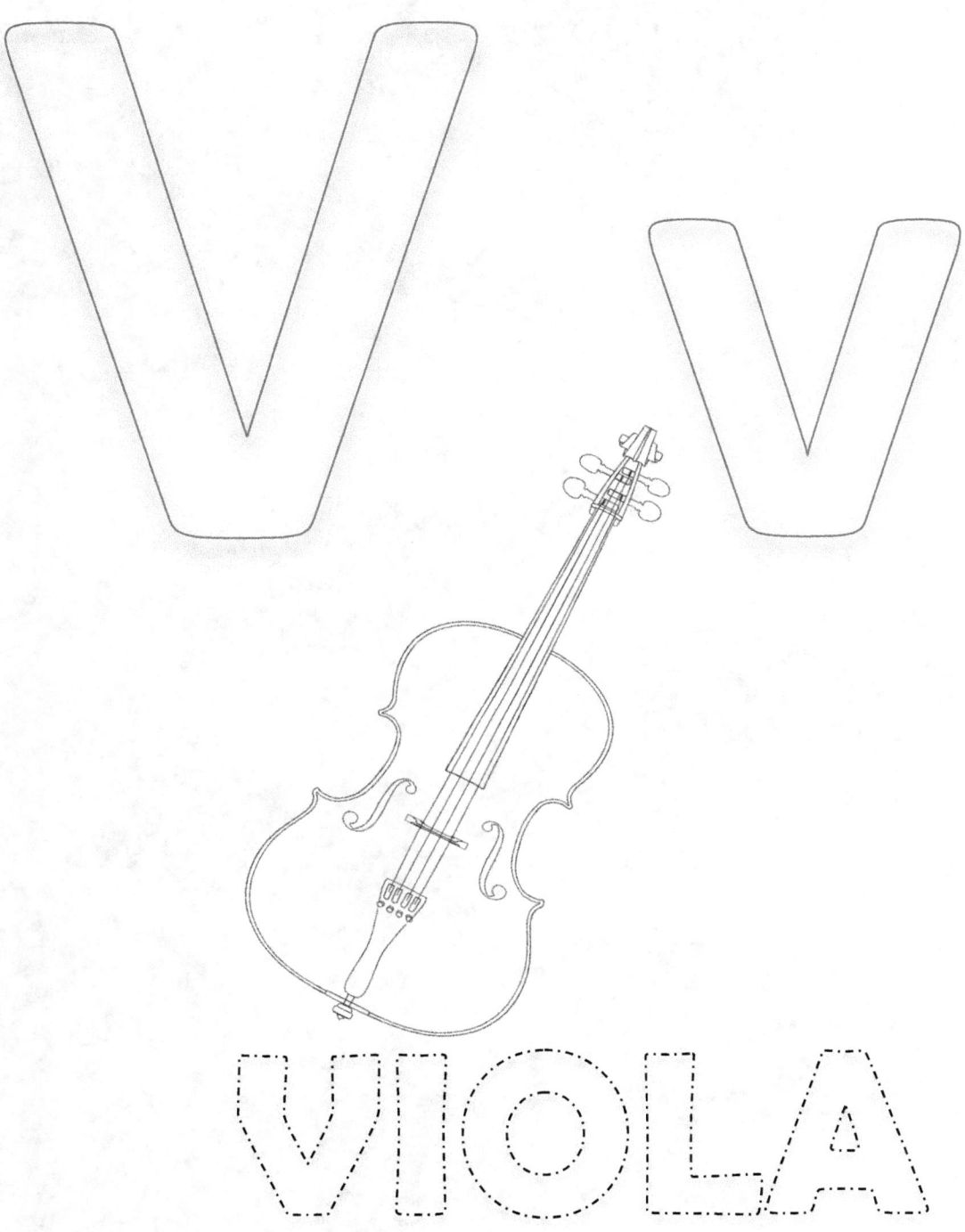

Ww

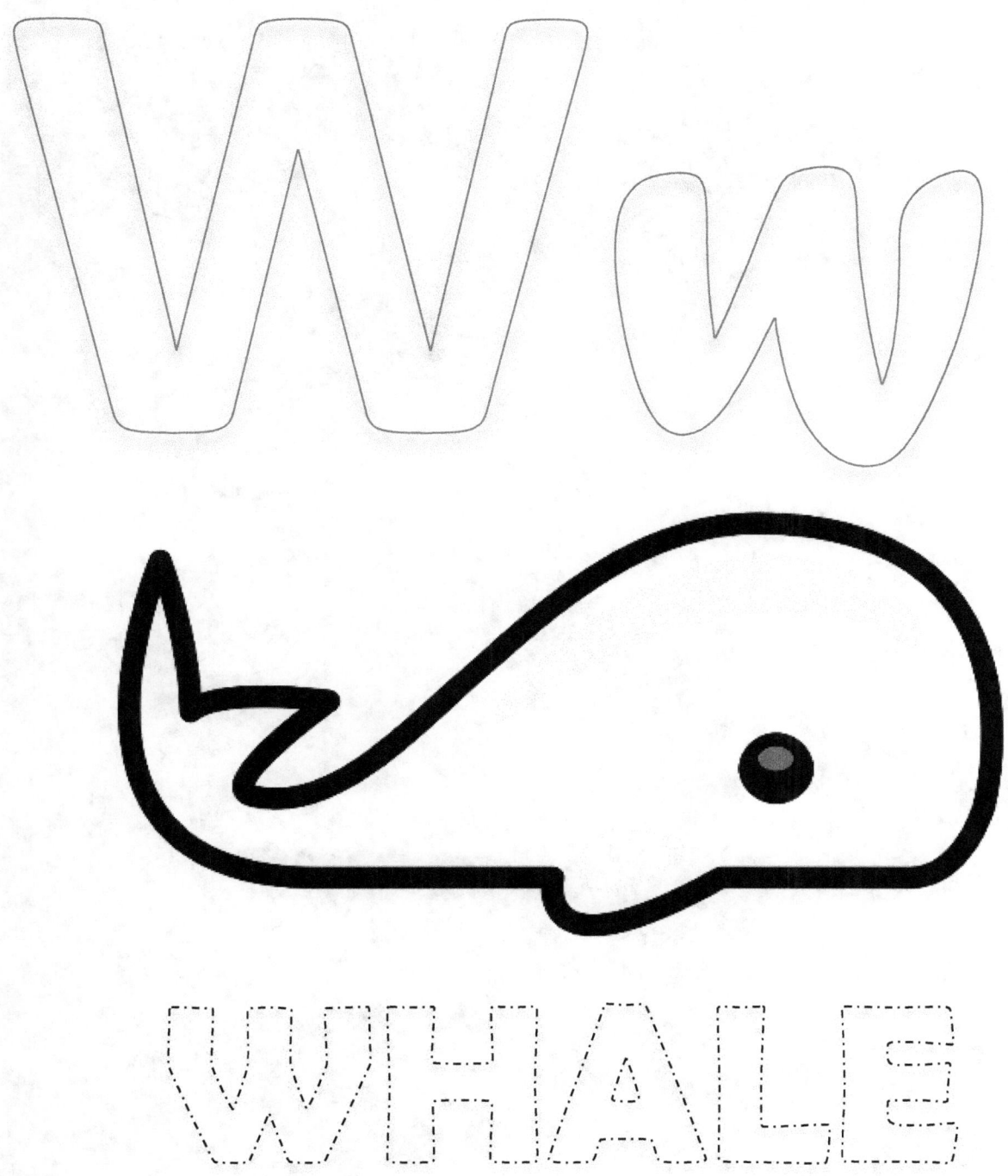

WHALE

X x

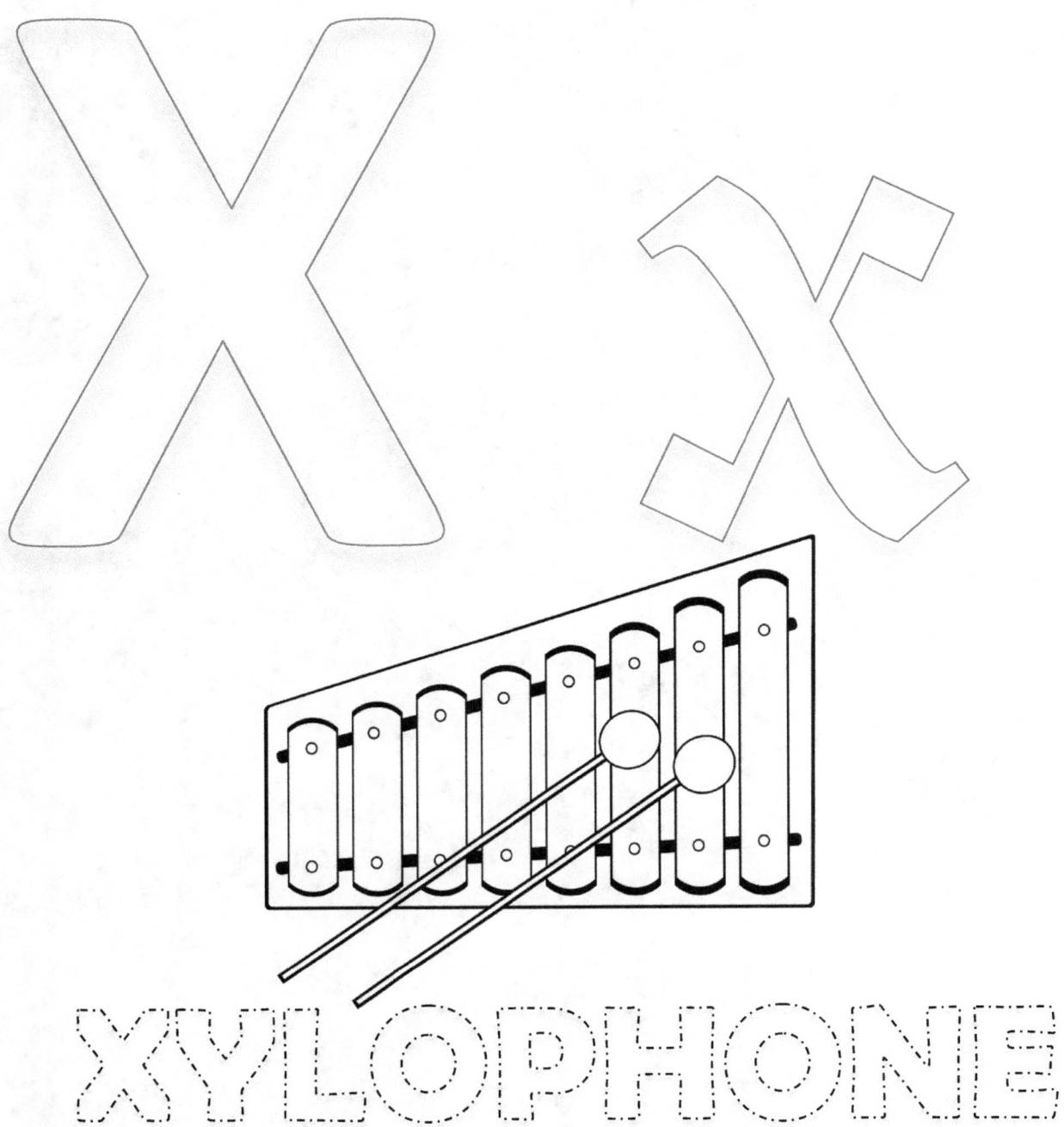

XYLOPHONE

Y y

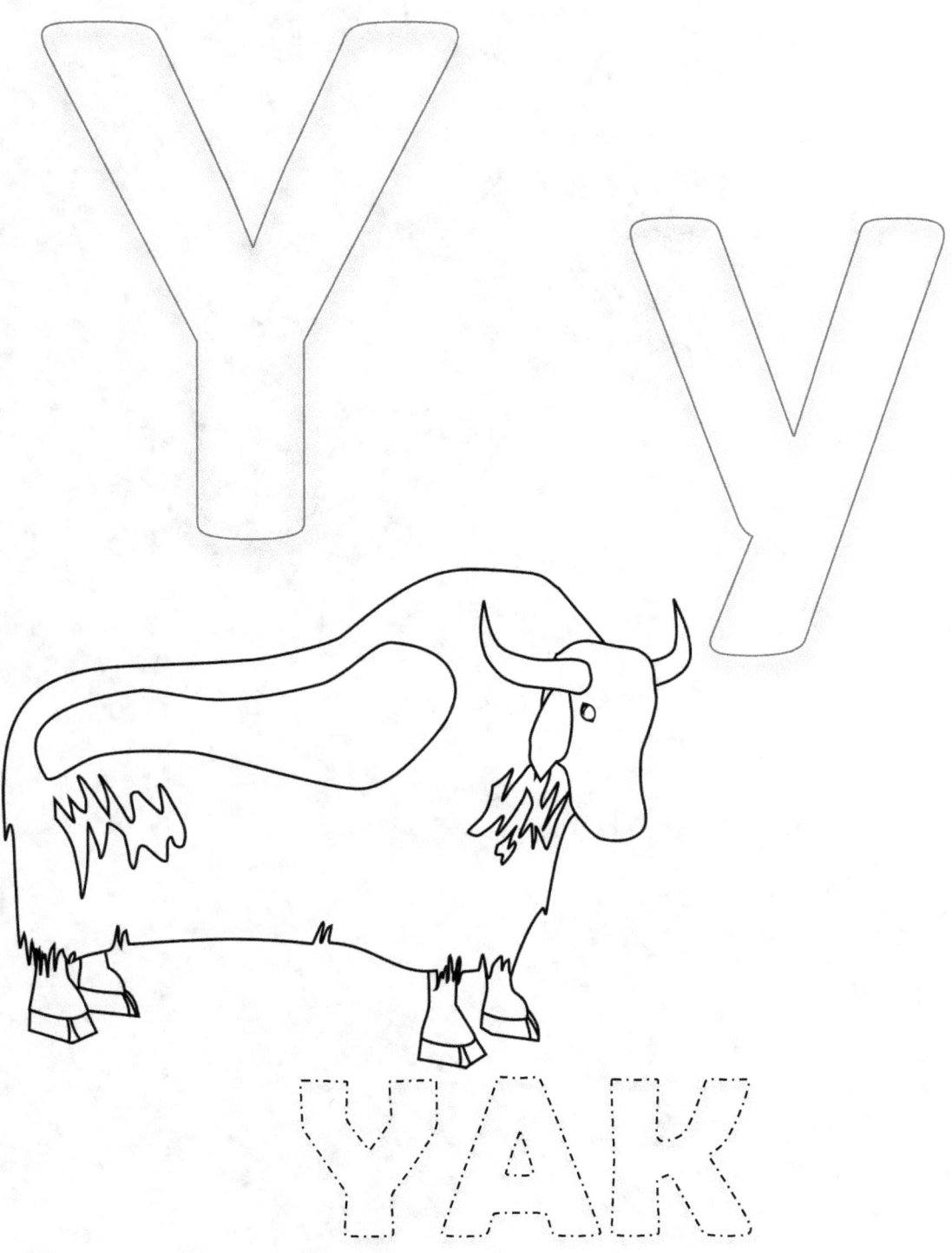

YAK

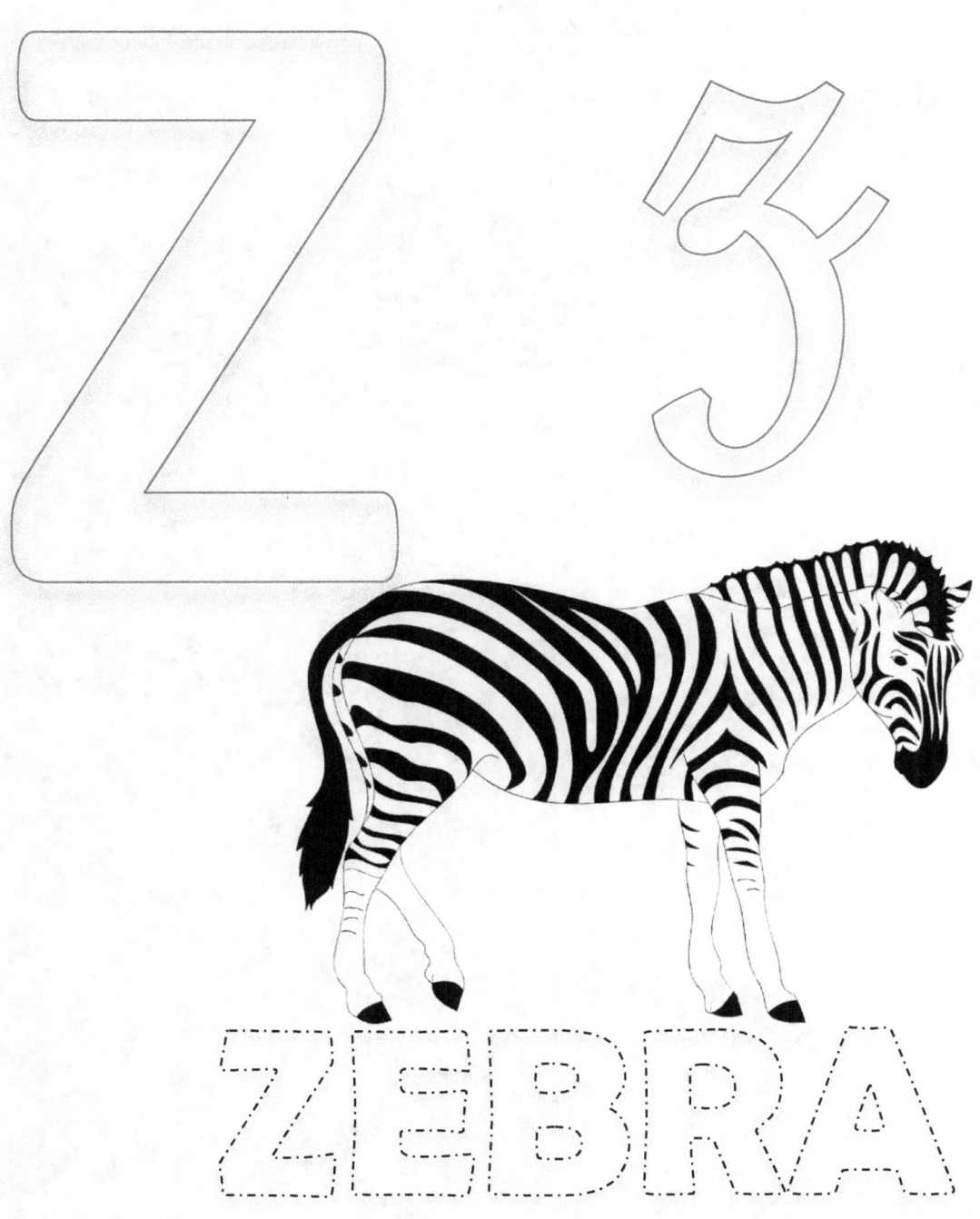

Matching fun

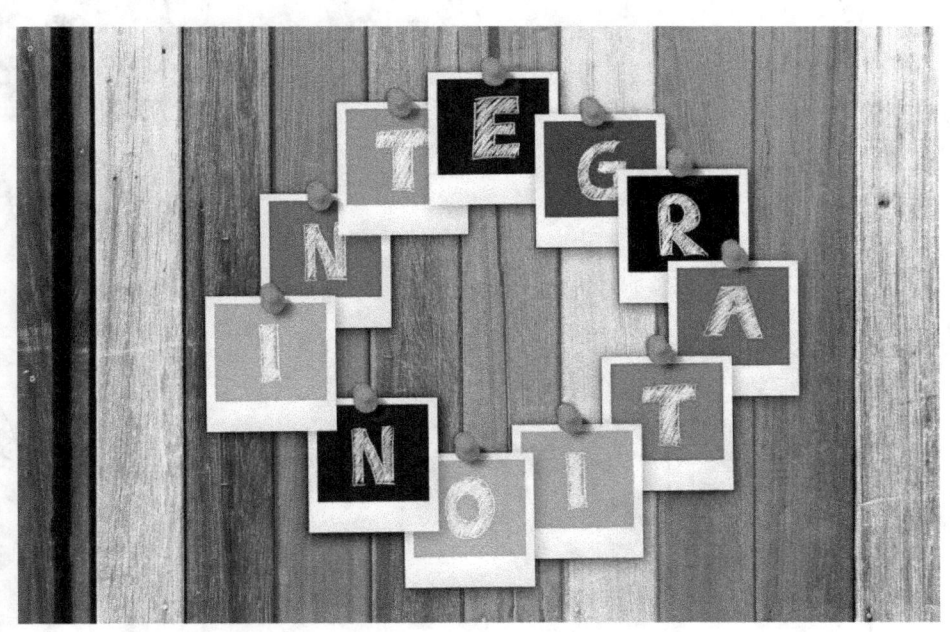

By Legend ART

APPLE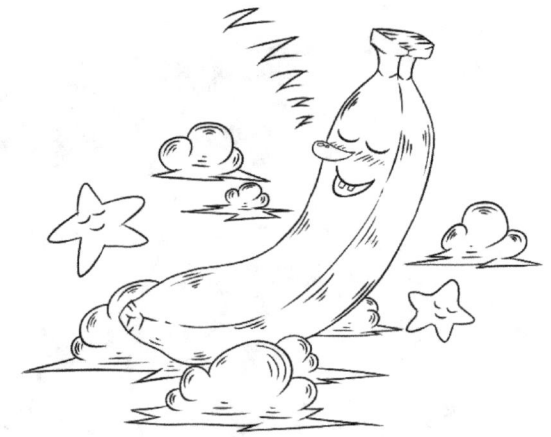

BANANA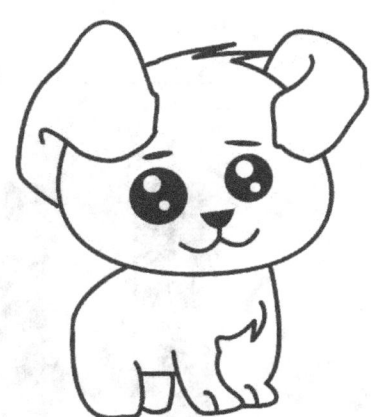

DOG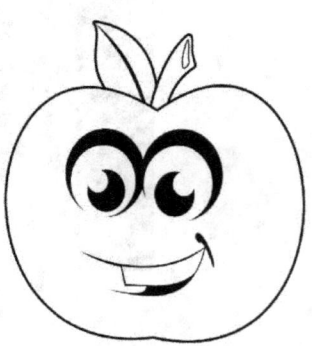

57

LION

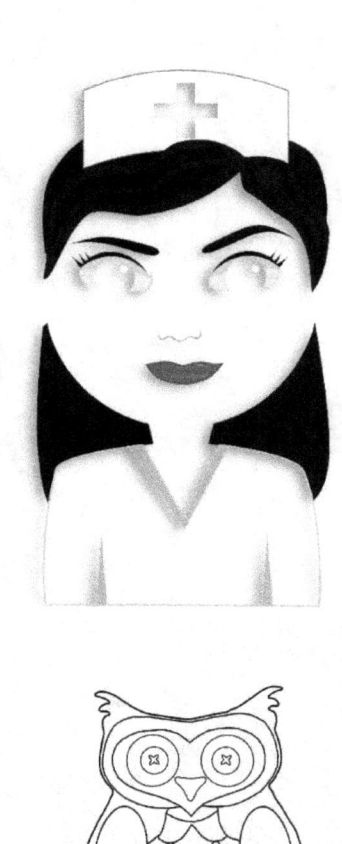

OWL

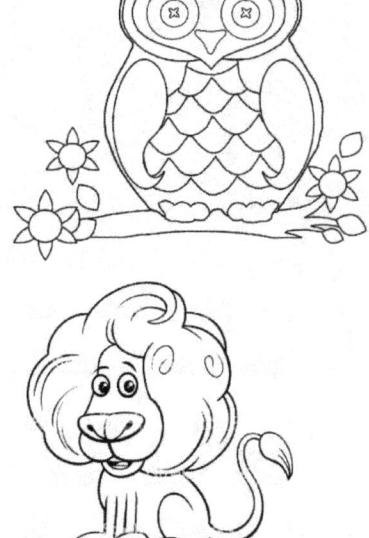

NURSE

ICEKREAM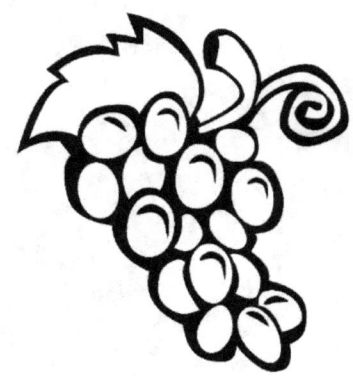

KITTEN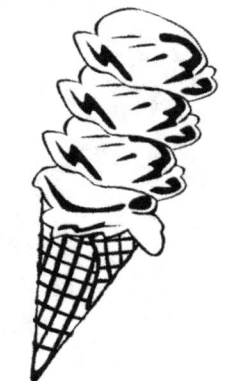

GRAPES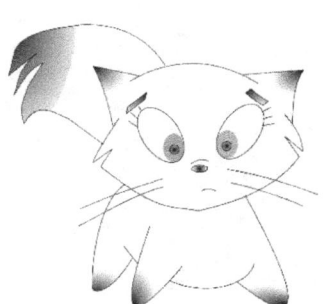

FISH

CHERRIES

ELEPHANT

VIOLA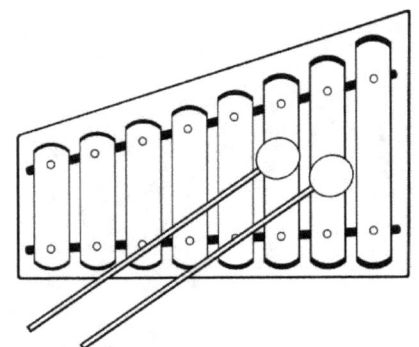

XYLOPHONE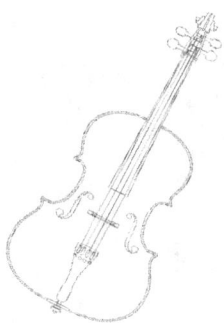

WHALE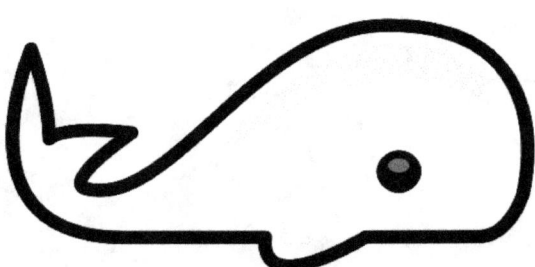

65

RAINBOW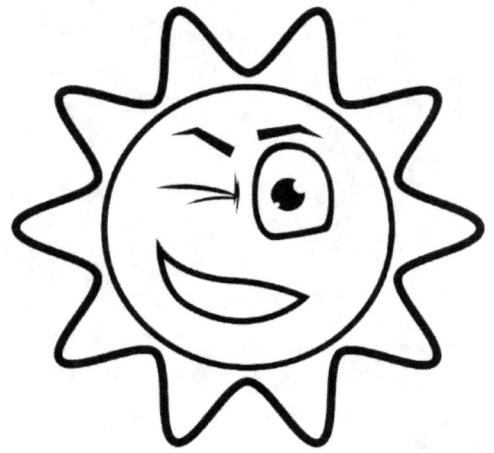

QUEEN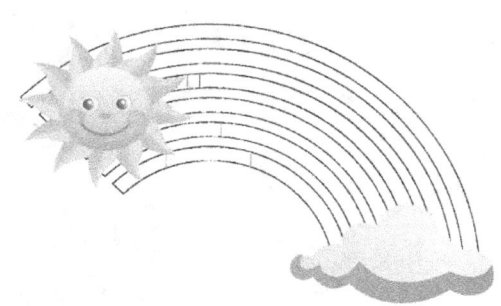

SUN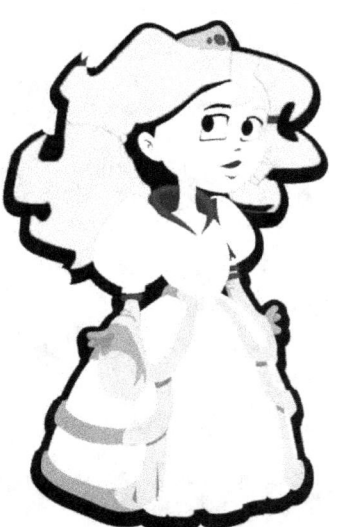

67

LOVE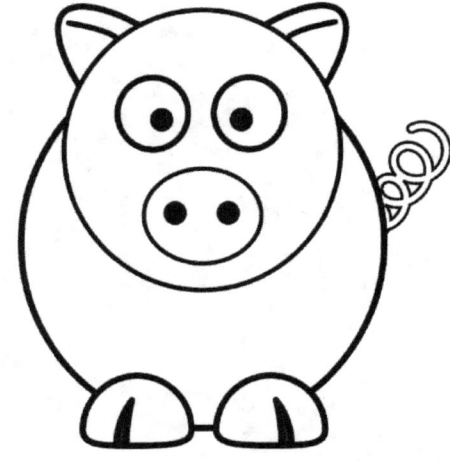

PIG

ZEBRA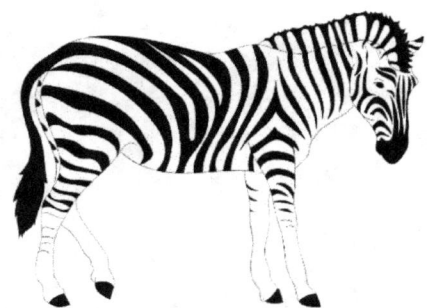

UMBRELLA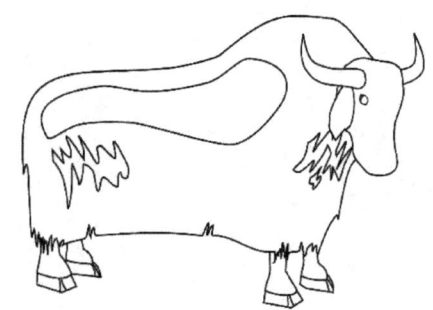

YAK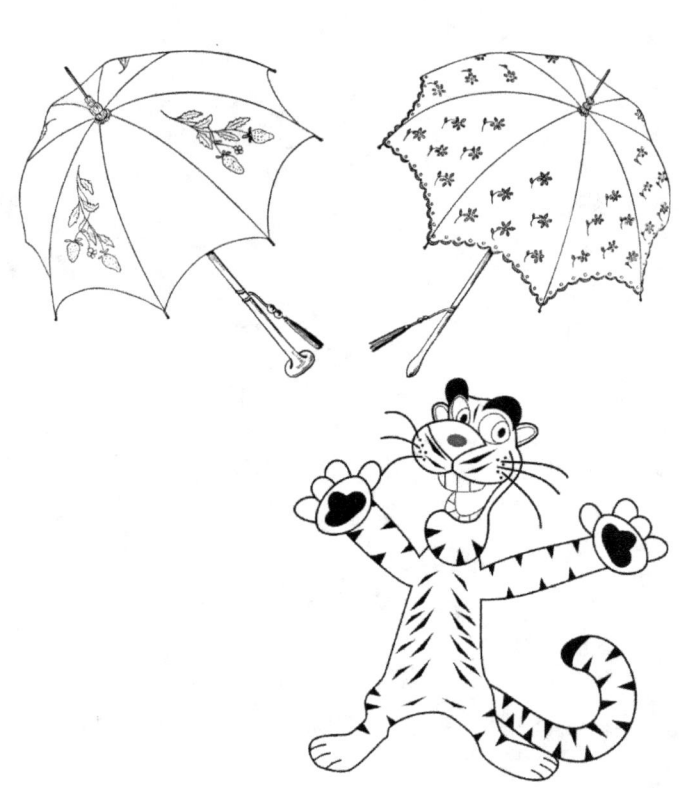

TIGER

JELLY

MOUSE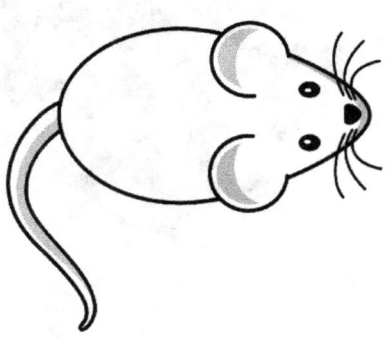

I AM A CHAMPION

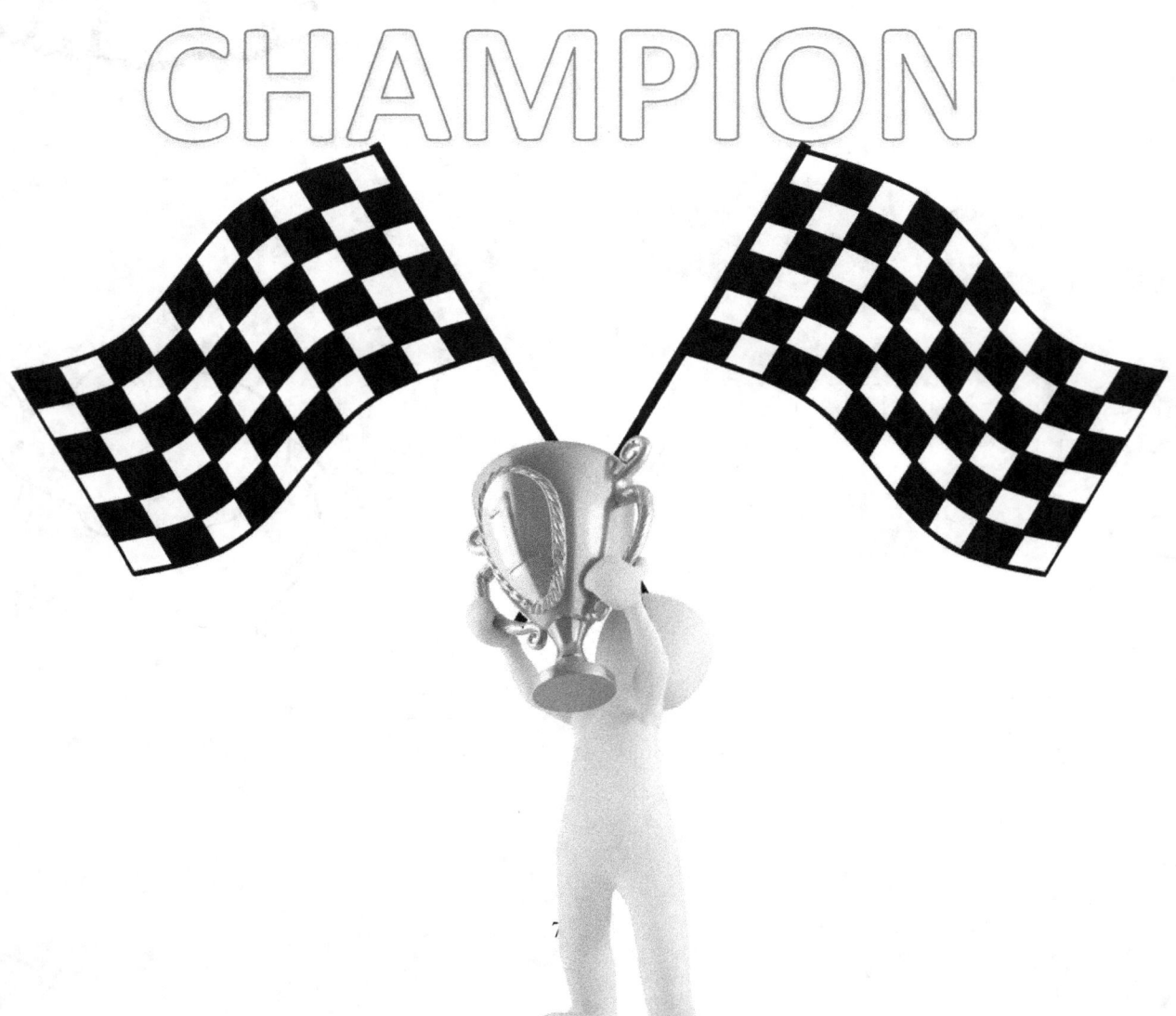